JANE FONDA

JANE FONDA

A BIOGRAPHY BY

SEAN FRENCH

PAVILION

First published in Great Britain in 1997 by
Pavilion Books Limited
London House
Great Eastern Wharf
Parkgate Road
London SW11 4NQ

Distributed in the U.S. by
Trafalgar Square Publishing
North Pomfret, Vermont 05053

Project Editor Tessa Clayton
Picture Researcher Linda Silverman
Indexer Valerie Chandler

Designed by Blackjacks

A CIP catalogue record for this book is available from the British Library

ISBN 1 85793 658 2

Printed and bound in Spain by Bookprint
Repro by D.P. Graphics, England

10 9 8 7 6 5 4 3 2 1

This book may be ordered by post direct from the publisher.
Please contact the Marketing Department. But try your bookshop first.

CONTENTS

INTRODUCTION

We make out of the quarrel with others, rhetoric,
but of the quarrel with ourselves, poetry.

W.B. Yeats

Do I contradict myself?
Very well then I contradict myself,
(I am large, I contain multitudes.)

Walt Whitman

For better or worse, Jane Fonda is the most important woman in the history of the cinema so far. This is a shocking statement, not because it is arguable but – on the contrary – because it is incontrovertible.

Her importance is of a particular kind. Famous and successful as she has been, she won't be remembered as one of the legends of the cinema. Jane Fonda hasn't become a part of our subconscious lives, the way that Marlene Dietrich and Greta Garbo have. She was striking looking in all sorts of different ways – wide-eyed and soft in *Barbarella*, sleek, bright in, say, *Julia* – but she didn't have the startling beauty of Ingrid Bergman or Elizabeth Taylor. She was sexy in the way that a leading actress has to be, but she always seemed a little amused by her own erotic image. Even when she was briefly,

The young Jane Fonda, moulded for movie stardom:
corset, tights and steely smile.

and factitiously, notorious for appearing nude in the films of her first husband, Roger Vadim, she was never a dream of carnality like the naked Brigitte Bardot or the fully clothed Rita Hayworth. Though Fonda was a resourceful performer, both in drama and comedy, she didn't have the uncanny gifts of a Carole Lombard or a Katharine Hepburn or a Judy Garland.

Yet she is a crucial figure in a way that none of them could rival. Through the circumstances of her birth and upbringing, and her own remarkable character, she seemed to understand what it meant to be a woman in Hollywood and she made use of that knowledge to take control of her career and achieve power in the industry. No actress had ever managed that before.

'All you need to make a film', said Jean-Luc Godard, 'is a girl and a gun.' In practice you could even dispense with the gun. The story of Hollywood – where the studios were run by men and the films were, overwhelmingly, produced, directed and written by men – could plausibly be told simply as an obsessed expression of the complicated adoration, lust, fear and hatred that men feel for women. The face of Ruby Keeler, the legs of Betty Grable, the hair of Veronica Lake. Women are the predators who lead men astray – Barbara Stanwyck in *Double Indemnity*, Joan Bennett in *Scarlet Street* – or the victim who gets stabbed to death in the shower. 'Make the woman suffer' was Alfred Hitchcock's self-confessed formula for suspense.

If Hollywood was an image on a screen, it was also an industry employing thousands of people and Jane Fonda, daughter of one of the most famous actors in the world, grew up knowing both sides intimately. It is no coincidence that her two finest performances are in more or less coded portrayals of the lives of failed screen actresses, in *They Shoot Horses, Don't They?* and *Klute*, and the humiliations and

The old Jane Fonda, the consort of an entertainment mogul
and still in the limelight: steely smile, steely dress.

depravities visited on them. During the golden age of Hollywood, the final years of which Fonda glimpsed as a child, aspiring actresses were subject to the most grievous forms of economic and sexual exploitation. The tiny elite of successful actresses may have been richer and better known, but they were exploited just the same and the only power they could exercise over their movie career was to leave it and do something else. 'I didn't say actors *were* cattle,' Alfred Hitchcock protested. 'I said they should be *treated* like cattle.' And they were. Their bodies were manipulated by diets, corsets and surgery. Young actresses like Judy Garland and Marilyn Monroe were drugged in order to keep their weight down, to wake them up, to get them to sleep, or simply to get through the punishing schedule dictated by the demands of the market. Actresses like Louise Brooks, Frances Farmer and Ann Dvorak, who tried to assert some sort of independence, saw their careers systematically destroyed. Sometimes, as with Garland and Monroe, the self-assertion was indistinguishable from mental illness caused by the practices of the industry that had made them famous.

˙Even the best-behaved actresses saw their careers fade as they moved through their thirties. Ingrid Bergman's Hollywood career was famously destroyed by the scandal of her adulterous affair with the Italian director, Roberto Rossellini, in 1949. But she was thirty-four, and her previous film, Hitchcock's *Under Capricorn*, had been a box-office flop. Rita Hayworth's elopement with Prince Aly Khan in the same year had the same effect but she had made three flops in a row and was thirty-one.

The actress's career would stall on the eve of middle age and those with marketable talents might find a career elsewhere: Katharine Hepburn on stage, Judy Garland and Marlene Dietrich as

Fonda: the new Bardot or an amused
all-American girl?

Jane Fonda inherited her father's blue eyes, firm jaw
and sense of purpose.

singers. One of the shrewdest of them all, Lucille Ball, went into television and ended up owning RKO, the studio that had once employed her. Some of them might return to the screen a few years later in character roles playing mothers and aunts. Men got off more lightly. 'You know what's wrong with you?' Audrey Hepburn famously asked Cary Grant in Stanley Donen's *Charade*. 'Nothing.' At the time he was seven years older than Bette Davis when she played the demented crone in *What Ever Happened to Baby Jane?*

Female movie stars were symbols of transcendent glamour who turned into equally symbolic victims of a culture that fetishises young female beauty. Most actresses began their career intoxicated by the first until they ran up against the second. Much of the drama of Jane Fonda's extraordinary life and career was fuelled by her knowledge of these two sides of the life almost from the beginning. 'I started late in the business, I was twenty-two,' she recalled, looking back when she was all of thirty. 'I realised early on that I didn't have the immediate striking beauty or a fixed unchanging film image. What I have is the intelligence and personality to be a star. I want the long haul, the long run.'

Already at an age when many female film stars' careers are all but over, Fonda was becoming aware of other younger actresses achieving success. Worse still, she seemed to have made some disastrously misguided career choices. Despite wanting to establish a new reputation as a serious dramatic actress, she had turned down what were probably the two finest Hollywood female roles of the sixties, in *Bonnie and Clyde* and *Rosemary's Baby*. And while these triumphs were making stars of Faye Dunaway (four years younger than Fonda) and Mia Farrow (eight years younger), Fonda was in Europe starring in *Barbarella*.

Fonda with Peter Finch in Greece in 1962 filming
In the Cool of the Day.

Yet from this low ebb – admittedly a low ebb of considerable international fame – she was to reinvent herself totally. She left her husband, her previous career, one might almost say her previous character. Three years later she had won the Oscar for best actress. Seven years after that she won it again for a film produced by her own company. She was a major force in the industry and that power fed back into her own career. It seemed as if she was able to embody a new positive image for middle-aged women. In her forties, and looking it, she was able to play leading roles in major Hollywood movies. When she partnered Robert Redford in *The Electric Horseman* in 1979, it was the first time Redford had starred opposite an actress of his own age since the two of them had acted together in *Barefoot in the Park*, twelve years earlier. But Fonda didn't start a trend, as she herself glumly observed: 'What I really hate is watching Robert Redford get younger and younger leading ladies. We're living in a society that makes it more difficult for women to get older than men. There is a definite double standard. Men get lines of distinction. Women get crow's feet.' Redford's last two co-stars, Demi Moore and Michelle Pfeiffer, are, respectively, twenty-five and twenty years younger than him.

Nevertheless, Fonda's middle-aged screen image fed triumphantly back into her business life. Screen actresses have always been treated like a commodity, but Jane Fonda was the first to market her brand name effectively. She lent her name and her energy to an exercise studio and the result was the greatest success of her career. The photograph of a striped, leotarded, grinning Fonda, legs askew, remains one of the defining images of the eighties. There had always been talk of the Fonda dynasty, though in reality it rarely amounted to more than a journalistic creation.

But now, from scratch, she had built a business empire whose main products were self-esteem, image, glamour and health, as packaged in a series of bestselling videos and books.

Her triumph seemed complete. The accusation made against Jane Fonda by amateur Freudians is that she has always been dependent on men because of the damage done to her by being the daughter of Henry Fonda, a man revered as an actor, coldly unresponsive as a father. Whether she was dependent on the men in her life or not, she had outstripped all of them, not least her first two husbands, Roger Vadim and Tom Hayden. For a brief period in the late sixties she had been eclipsed by her brother, Peter, whose *Easy Rider* (which he starred in and produced) had made him famous and rich. By the late eighties, he was less famous than his daughter, Bridget, let alone his sister. Above all, perhaps, she was a match for her father. She would never attain his mythic status, but she won more Oscars than he did ('lifetime achievement' Oscars don't count). Sweeter still, his one acting Oscar was in a film that she had produced, and *she* picked it up for him.

If this were all, she would merely be a figure of immense cultural importance, revered for her contributions to various branches of the leisure and entertainment industry. But it isn't all. 'I've had the most interesting life of any human being I know,' Jane Fonda said as she looked back from the vantage point of her late fifties. It's a plausible contention.

Most actors don't lead very interesting lives. They may have a lot of sex, take drugs, drink, go to parties. Some follow praiseworthy second careers as goodwill ambassadors for children's charities. But most of their professional lives are spent on film sets and on location waiting in their trailers while lights are arranged and sets

A notorious image of Fonda, a poster bought by her fans for
their bedroom walls and by her enemies for their placards.

adjusted. And except for a few stalkers and autograph hounds, the public's emotions towards film stars are relatively restrained. Occasionally, the film audience, or its representatives, will show dislike or disapproval of a performer. Katharine Hepburn and Marlene Dietrich were notoriously pronounced 'box-office poison' by a US exhibitors' association in the late thirties.

Jane Fonda is different. Many actors have been involved on the margins of politics, but few have progressed beyond attending rallies, making donations and informing on their colleagues. Fonda, by contrast, has never been half-hearted in any of her activities. The result of this commitment has varied from the absurd to the magnificent, but her involvement in the protests against the Vietnam war had more serious implications. In the summer of 1972 she visited Hanoi, the capital of North Vietnam, with her then new partner, Tom Hayden. What would have happened if Rita Hayworth had visited Berlin in 1944 and called on allied soldiers to desert? There remains a significant number of people who believe that Jane Fonda should have been indicted for treason.

Her reputation at the height of her business success in the mid-eighties was unparalleled. She was a dominant figure in the development of a leisure industry aimed specifically at women, a role model for millions, while another group, mainly composed of war veterans and their families, still believed that President Nixon should have had her executed when he had the chance. And the bitterness has refused to fade. Even in the eighties, any business activity or filming in a public place was liable to be disrupted by placard-waving demonstrators.

But Jane Fonda has always moved more quickly than her enemies or her allies. Time and commercial imperatives have

Jane Fonda with her first husband, Roger Vadim:
who was using whom?

Her father's daughter: Fonda put on a cowboy hat for
Cat Ballou (1965).

Hollywood acceptance: Fonda in 1972 with Gene
Hackman, Cloris Leachman and her Oscar for *Klute*.

proved more difficult to evade. Jane Fonda had been articulate about the problems of growing older: 'To be a mid-life woman in our society is to be a pioneer. The middle years for women represent virtually unexplored territory.' And it wasn't just talk. Whatever their other qualities, films like *Julia* and *Coming Home* showed that a forty-year-old woman could be the heroine of a Hollywood movie, which was arguably more radical than anything else about them. For a while there was a hope that she might do the same thing, even more radically, for old age. As she put it in one of her books, anticipating her own future: 'I see an old woman walking briskly out of doors, in every season. She's feisty. She's not afraid of being alone. Her face is lined and full of life. She likes to be with young people, and she's a good listener. Her grandchildren love to tell her stories and to hear hers because she's got some really good ones that contain sweet, hidden lessons about life.' She called on women to make friends with their wrinkles.

Fonda was always a powerful proponent of the view that the Hollywood system was biased against women. The discrimination against middle-aged women was even more severe, and she combated it with brilliant success. In the end, however, she ran up against an immovable barrier: the Hollywood prejudice against middle-aged women whose films lose money. In the eight years after the triumph of *On Golden Pond*, she made five flops in a row, poorly reviewed flops at that. Not even Jane Fonda could survive that.

Indeed she hasn't made a film since, and it raised issues about her career as a whole. What had been the effect of Fonda's activism, both for herself and more generally? How had she developed as an actress? What was the relationship between her art and her politics?

Jane Fonda in *Steelyard Blues* (1973): funny,
eccentric, risky and a flop.

Fonda with Ted Turner: at sixty she is reinventing herself once more as one half of the ultimate power couple.

How had they defined each other? And since it coincided with the acrimonious breakdown of her marriage to Tom Hayden, it posed a more pressing question for Fonda herself: what was she to do with the rest of her life?

Robert Redford once described her as a phoenix who always rises from the ashes. The image may be hackneyed, but it was scarcely avoidable. In 1986, a year after her criticisms of cosmetic surgery, Fonda had cosmetic surgery involving the removal of fat from her upper and lower eyelids. Then in February 1987 she had breast implants. After the final break with Tom Hayden, she had a couple of avowedly transitional affairs and then began a very public relationship with Ted Turner, the founder of CNN, a man who was wealthier and more powerful than she was, and nearly as famous.

A phoenix had been consumed: there were ashes and something was emerging from them, but it seemed like a different bird altogether. Jane Fonda gave up her work – 'Ted was real upfront. He said: "I need you here."' She renounced her feminism, just as she had earlier renounced her political radicalism. As if this wasn't disturbing enough, she claimed that she had even been wrong about aerobics: 'I was hopelessly addicted to exercise . . . I wanted the relationship with Ted to work, which meant I couldn't spend so much time exercising.' And in case there was any doubt that those old bestselling videos were mistaken, she had a new video to prove it.

Her film career had stalled, her radical political project had failed, her health advice was all wrong. Roger Vadim's career had evaporated. Who, outside California, knew what Tom Hayden was up to? Yet here was Jane Fonda approaching sixty, more visible than ever. Perhaps that was the greatest triumph of all.

Chapter One

HENRY
& JANE

The first time that Jane Fonda congratulated her father on a screen performance was in 1969 when she was thirty-one and he was sixty-four. She was newly confident. Starring in *They Shoot Horses, Don't They?*, she had finally and unequivocally established her reputation as a serious dramatic actress, and she had been rewarded with an Oscar nomination. Nevertheless, her father's role was something special.

Almost from the beginning of his career, there had been an air of sanctity attached to the name of Henry Fonda. In his mid-thirties, his persona was defined forever by two famous performances in John Ford movies: as *Young Mr Lincoln* in 1939 and as Tom Joad in *The Grapes of Wrath* the following year. They were classic incarnations of American decency: understated, essentially rural, a self-made nobility, modest yet utterly secure in its

Henry Fonda and daughter pose dutifully for the camera:
she looks cool, he looks frosty.

sense of what is right, independent to the point of being untouch-able and alone.

Henry Fonda inspired the kind of respect that was more usually accorded to distinguished elder statesmen, and this may have constrained him in the kind of roles he felt able to accept. James Stewart and John Wayne, both close friends of Fonda, also had established screen personas but in their finest roles were able to show the conflict, anxiety, even madness beneath the heroic exteriors of their characters. By contrast, Fonda was always unruffled, even a little staid. His best films explored or mocked this stiffness. In *The Lady Eve*, Preston Sturges shrewdly cast Barbara Stanwyck opposite him to goad and taunt him into life.

Wasn't there something chilling about an actor who required such security of character? Take one of his most popular films, and the only one he produced himself, Sidney Lumet's *Twelve Angry Men* (1957). It is one of the great expressions of liberal civic responsibility. As a jury member, Fonda leads eleven of his fellow citizens to rise above their prejudices and acquit a boy accused of a murder he didn't commit. In its use of the confinement of the jury room and the process by which the jurors are convinced one by one, the film is almost irresistible but not quite. Within the limits of the slightly glib script, each of the characters is probed, exposed and changed, all except one: Henry Fonda's character, Davis, the architect. Even the profession is emblematic. In 1957 architects were the people who were solving poor people's problems by knocking down the areas where they lived and replacing them with clear, logical housing developments where they could live healthy, responsible lives.

Most of us don't believe in architects as benevolent social engineers any more and, likewise, as the years go by we enjoy *Twelve*

Henry Fonda (1905–1982), the most respected of Hollywood movie stars.

Jane Fonda was born into the Hollywood aristocracy, a society she had mixed feelings about from the beginning.

Angry Men not as political realism but as glorious melodramatic hokum, in which Fonda's sense of his own impregnable virtue is part of the pleasure but as artificial as a pirouette by Fred Astaire.

Like many actors, Fonda eased into old age with a series of slack character roles. When, in the late sixties, he was offered a role in a Western to be filmed in Europe he contemptuously rejected it and was only persuaded to change his mind by his friend Eli Wallach, who had worked with Sergio Leone before. Leone had an ornate Italian style and a deep feeling for American movies. He liked American actors, but was intelligent and fresh in his use of them. He had already brought over an American TV cowboy, told him to stop acting and keep silent, and turned Clint Eastwood into the biggest star in the world.

Fonda was playing the villain in Leone's film *Once Upon a Time in the West*, so he grew a beard for the part and wore brown contact lenses to cover the blue eyes that, in the iconography of American film, belonged to presidents and sheriffs. In his own words: 'When I walked onto the set, Sergio, who spoke no English, took one look at me and let loose a volley of rapid-fire Italian, gesturing wildly with his hands and arms as he spoke. An interpreter stood beside him, and the first word in English I heard was "Shave!" And the next thing was, "Throw away the brown eyes. Where are the big blues? That's what I bought."'

Early in *Once Upon a Time in the West* a family is seen outside their ranch house on the prairie laying a table for a ceremonial meal. Suddenly there is a gunshot and one of the children falls to the ground, then the father, then another child. All the family is dead except for one small boy. From behind we see gunmen, in those long coats known as dusters, walking forward towards him. The camera moves slowly around and we see that the leader of the murderers is Henry Fonda. 'What'll we do with this one, Frank?' one of his associates asks. Fonda spits into the dirt. 'Well, now that you called me by my name . . .' And he pulls a gun and shoots the little boy.

It is one of the great raucously shocking moments of cinema and yet it is more than just coarse casting against type. Leone had a peerless eye for surfaces, for landscapes and faces, and he had evidently seen that there was a coldness in Henry Fonda's jewelled blue eyes, that his imperturbability might be an expression of emotional nullity. It is difficult not to believe that Jane Fonda congratulated her father because he had shown his dark side on screen for the first time in his career.

Once Upon a Time in the West was a success all over the world, except in the United States where it failed disastrously. There were various explanations for this but one of the most plausible was that American filmgoers were simply not willing to see a scary Henry Fonda (or, more likely, that US exhibitors were incapable of believing that they were). For his children, however, this was less of a surprise. They had lived with the paradox all their lives.

Jane Fonda was born on 21 December 1937, the first child of Henry Fonda, who at thirty-two was on the brink of becoming one of the major leading men in Hollywood. He had been briefly married before, to the actress Margaret Sullavan, who went on to marry Leland Hayward, his manager and best friend. His second wife had nothing to do with show business. On a voyage to England in 1936, he had met a recently widowed socialite, Frances Seymour Brokaw. She was from the American upper class, but the family's wealth had largely been squandered by her alcoholic father. She had also married an alcoholic who drowned while drunk in the swimming pool of the

Jane Fonda: an East Coast sensibility inside a
West Coast body.

sanatorium where he was supposedly being cured. Henry Fonda, the symbol of stability and reason, seems always to have gravitated towards eccentricity, chaos, madness, as if he were seeking out people who expressed what he kept hidden.

Frances showed no attraction for the film business, or for the social life that surrounded it, nor did she show any interest in her new daughter. She had wanted a boy, and Jane Fonda has never pretended that there was much of a bond between them. On 23 February 1940 Frances had a son, and he was named Peter. As it turned out, Frances would be no more affectionate to her son than she was to her daughter. Instead, she devoted herself obsessively to managing her husband's money. His earnings were substantial enough, but he was under contract to Daryl Zanuck and the amount he earned was far less than what successful stars would earn in later decades when they were independent and could demand higher fees as well as a percentage of what their films earned.

Much later, an anonymous business associate of Jane would say of her background: 'You can't fully understand Jane unless you know something about the California upper class. It's not like back East, the New York and Boston closed society that produced Katharine Hepburn. Jane is a younger, palm-tree version of Hepburn. A jock, an athlete, incredibly strong for a woman. A tomboy.'

This is to oversimplify. Jane's mother was from precisely that East Coast upper-class society and she had a disdain for the vulgar Beverly Hills existence that her daughter inherited. Henry Fonda grew up in Omaha, Nebraska and his languid Midwestern drawl was maintained, almost as a sign of his integrity. Jane has characterised him as 'a mid-westerner by birth and by nature'. He had a touch of the East Coast about him as well. He made his name in the theatre

The Fondas read a script together: in reality, Henry gave his
daughter his looks and his contacts, but little encouragement.

and it always remained a creative and emotional refuge when the film industry failed him.

Jane and Peter Fonda grew up as the children of a rich and very famous father. Their home life was elegant, if less ostentatious than that of many of their friends, and they were educated at expensive, socially exclusive private schools. Unquestionably they were in Hollywood's upper class, but unlike many film stars, Henry Fonda had the social confidence of somebody who inhabited other worlds as well. He didn't have Katharine Hepburn's contempt for the film industry, but he had a sense of perspective about it and his career and this was always to influence his daughter. As she recalled, 'I have seen from my life at home how unhappy so many stars were and why so many of their lives have been tragedies. My father has lasted in Hollywood because he doesn't panic, or change or cheapen himself. He goes in a certain direction unhesitatingly.'

They were geographically separate from the film community as well, even when they were living in California. Jane has described the home where she lived until she was ten as 'a sort of farm in the foothills of the Santa Monica Mountains overlooking the Pacific Ocean'. This may give a misleading impression – the estate contained vegetable gardens, chickens and horses, but also tennis courts, a pool and a large staff including maids, cooks, governesses and a gardener.

The problems of growing up in Hollywood are as well known as the wealth and glamour. The clash between the world-famous idealised image on the screen and the imperfect flawed person behind it would be pressure enough to test the strongest personality and the most loving family. This disparity takes many forms. In Henry Fonda's case, the contrast between the stately gentleness of the image and the harshness of the man was especially disturbing for those close to him. By all accounts, he could be generous and charming in social situations, but he could also be manipulative and cold with his family, friends and close colleagues. Perhaps in response to personal suffering, such as the brief disaster of his first marriage, he adopted a stoical personality that could seem merely unaffectionate and undemonstrative. He was never openly loving with his children, and his temper, either at work or at home, was legendary. 'His rages were terrifying,' Jane later said.

In the introduction to a cookbook published when Jane was in her late fifties, she recalled with nostalgia life on the Californian 'farm' where she grew up, the vegetables, fruit trees, the rabbit and chicken coop: 'To this day, I harbour a special fondness for fresh soft-boiled eggs.' She doesn't mention the occasion when the family dog, a Dalmatian, killed one of the chickens. As a punishment, Henry tied the dead body to the dog's collar and the poor mutt had to drag it round until it rotted away and disintegrated.

This alternation between coldness and capricious rage marked both of his children in different ways. Peter suffered more painfully, torn for the rest of his father's life between defying him and trying to emulate him, frequently doing both at the same time. In late middle age he was still asking the then elderly Henry for a direct emotional engagement that he wasn't willing to give. 'I dig my father,' he once said pathetically. 'I wish he could open his eyes and dig me.' The effect on Jane was less direct. Perhaps she had the stronger character, and she was a woman and did not have the immediate pressure to live up to her father's image of silent masculinity. But the influence was still strong. Interviewed at the age of twenty-eight, she looked back with painful clarity:

I was plump and graceless and lonely as a child, with a face like a chipmunk. I was shy and people thought I'd be pretty square when I grew up. Now I have changed – although I still don't think I have much of a face: just good eyes and then sort of nothing. The change isn't the power of positive thinking. It is like a computer. You feed in a series of goals and work toward them. I have.

There are two sorts of people in this world. The dead – even if they think they're living – and the survivors. We're survivors – all my family is. I'm not particularly European in that. I'm American – and just smart.

Jane's perception of herself as plump was intensified because it provoked a rare direct response from her father. Years later, when she was in her late teens and beginning to work as an actress, she visited her father who was then married to his fourth wife, Afdera, a young Italian woman scarcely older than Jane. The problematic influence Henry exercised on Jane can nowhere be seen more clearly than in Henry's own view of the event, as it is described in *Fonda, My Life*, the curious mixture of biography and memoir on which he collaborated with Howard Teichmann:

When [Jane] spent the summer with Henry and Afdera in Villefranche, she appeared in a bikini one day. Her father, noticing the skimpy bathing suit and his daughter's generous figure, casually advised the teen-aged girl not to wear anything so tight. That was enough for Jane. That and peer pressure did the trick. From then on Jane went on a series of sensible diets. To this day she eats sparingly and works out regularly and strenuously.

The teenage Jane Fonda: 'A jock, an athlete, incredibly
strong for a woman. A tomboy.'

It could probably be argued that in exacerbating his daughter's self-consciousness about her supposed weight problem, Henry Fonda was only reflecting typical attitudes towards women's bodies in the United States of the 1950s. But it is at the very least ironic, if not compelling evidence of his emotional detachment from his daughter, that even in old age he could assert that his advice, with peer pressure, 'did the trick' and that it had beneficially influenced her to go on 'a series of sensible diets'. Until her thirties, Jane suffered from bulimia, hence her 'sensible' diets consisted of habitually making herself vomit after eating. Her 1996 cookbook, *Cooking for Healthy Living*, contains a valuable page devoted to eating disorders. 'Anorexia and bulimia are illnesses,' she writes. 'They are not signs of moral weakness or character flaws. They are not who you are, but something that may have happened to you.' She assures the reader that the cycle of damaging behaviour can be broken and the bulimic can learn to eat in an anxiety-free way. She concludes with stark honesty: 'In time, she (or he) can assume a more spontaneous relationship with a variety of foods and with normal weight. I know because I did.'

Outwardly, Jane's childhood must have seemed ideally privileged, with her horses and her expensive schools. If there was a certain detachment from her father, then wasn't that only to be expected when he was absent for years serving in the US Navy during the Second World War, an experience shared by a generation of children?

When he returned from military service, Henry Fonda was even less inclined to resume his career as an indentured contract star. In 1948, after half a dozen movies – most notably John Ford's *My Darling Clementine* and *Fort Apache* – he took the name part of a play about a modestly heroic naval officer, *Mister Roberts*. The play ran for years on Broadway and the family moved back East.

Frances had become steadily more depressed, suffering from a variety of neurotic ailments as her husband had withdrawn from her. In 1949 he fell in love with Susan Blanchard, the twenty-one-year-old stepdaughter of the lyricist Oscar Hammerstein, and told Frances he wanted a divorce. This accelerated her mental problems and in 1950 she was committed to a psychiatric clinic. On 14 April, her forty-second birthday, she killed herself by cutting her throat with a razor.

Jane once paid an ambiguous compliment to her father, saying that he did 'things as an actor that I couldn't do. He played on stage in *Mister Roberts* for four years. His wife died during that time, and other personal tragedies came in his life. But there's not one person who won't say that he was just as good on closing night as opening night. I could never do that.' (Notice that 'his wife' rather than 'my mother'. Jane was always the daughter of Henry, not of Frances.) Henry told Jane, aged twelve, and Peter, aged ten, that their mother had died of a heart attack and then he drove to the theatre in New York City and, against the advice of his friends and colleagues, played Mr Roberts.

Just a few weeks later, Jane learned the truth about her mother's death in a profile of her father in a fan magazine. She was greatly distressed, but at the same time oddly detached. Interviewed in her mid-fifties, Jane recalled her mother as an example of the problem of women whose lives are devoted to beauty and wealth: 'She came originally from a poor family but she was beautiful and, when she lost her youth and her looks and she became paranoid about losing her money, she had nothing else. She just shrivelled up. There was no emotional stability to hold it all together. And there are many women like that.' Jane Fonda would never allow herself to be one of them. It was her younger brother who was more obviously traumatised. On 28 December 1950, Henry Fonda and Susan Blanchard were married and immediately departed on a honeymoon in the Virgin Islands. Two days later, Peter almost died of a self-inflicted gunshot wound, in what what was either an accident or an extreme attempt at attracting his father's notice. Peter himself has told it both ways and even his sister wasn't sure: 'Maybe it was an extravagant, romantic way of attracting attention,' she said later. 'I really don't know. Peter is a complex man and he needed love.' Peter recalled Henry coming back from the Virgin Islands '*very* angry that I ruined his honeymoon.' Despite injuries to the liver and a kidney, he survived. Peter would remain as divided and desperate as ever in his relationship with his father, but he was now closer to his sister. More surprisingly, he and Jane became close to their new stepmother, who was less than ten years older than them, and far more emotionally demonstrative than their mother (let alone their father) had been. Susan adored both Peter and Jane and responded to their emotional hunger. Cruelly, it was Henry's coldness that she found impossible to bear and that would break up their marriage after five years.

The one obvious sign of disorder in Jane's life was the bulimia from which she began to suffer as a teenager at Emma Wilward, an expensive boarding school in upstate New York. She, along with other friends, would eat large amounts of rich, sweet food and then make themselves sick. Otherwise her school career was successful and pleasingly unremarkable. She did well enough to go to Vassar, the prestigious women's college, where she showed a new independence, leading a hedonistic, sexually active life, though it may have been a search for affection, rather than pleasure. An early boyfriend would later remember her as 'so insecure and hungry for love that she tried to swallow you whole.' After two years of this, she left and went to Paris with vague aspirations to study art. 'I went to Paris to be a painter,' she later recalled. 'But I lived there for six months and never picked up a brush.' She had even more fun in Paris, largely with a group of young Americans associated with the literary journal, *The Paris Review*. Even though he was distracted with his new association with Afdera Franchetti (who, at twenty-four, was even younger than Susan Blanchard), Henry heard about Jane's behaviour and ordered her back to America.

On her last night in Paris, Jane went to a party at Maxim's and was introduced by her date, Christian Marquand, to Roger Vadim. She was already well aware of Vadim's reputation, not least because Christian Marquand had acted in Vadim's most famous film, *And God Created Woman*. The meeting passed quickly and insignificantly. After all, the two had little to offer each other. What could Fonda expect from Vadim, who was at the party with his latest blonde lover, Annette Strøyberg? Why should Vadim be interested in Henry Fonda's spoiled daughter who had been misbehaving in Paris?

Jane returned to New York City in disgrace and half-heartedly resumed piano and painting lessons. She had no other ambitions, but she also became friends with Susan Strasberg, an actress of her own age who was co-starring on stage with Henry Fonda. Jane had done some acting while at school and at college and nothing since. But Strasberg persuaded her to audition for classes with her father, Lee Strasberg, the most famous and influential acting teacher in America. His 'Method' style of acting, inspired by Konstantin

Stanislavsky's teachings and based on painstakingly prepared details of character supported by emotional truth, was part of a transformation of American performance style, most famously with such actors as Marlon Brando, James Dean and Paul Newman.

This young woman who was apparently nothing more than the fun-loving, pampered daughter of a Hollywood star, a college drop-out with no training and no apparent interest in the theatre, can't have seemed a very promising candidate for the Actors Studio. But beneath the fluffy exterior were the sensations of pain, anxiety and conflict that the Method, with its psychoanalytic use of personal experience, valued so highly. 'The only reason I took her was her eyes,' Lee Strasberg said later. 'There was such panic in her eyes.'

Chapter Two

ROGER S VERSION

J ane Fonda said that her life was changed utterly when she was praised by Lee Strasberg: 'Nobody had ever told me that I was ever good at anything.' She had found a father who said nice things to her and she liked it. This was fortunate because her real father seemed indifferent to her new choice of a career and openly contemptuous, like many older actors, of the Method. Nevertheless, whether he wanted to or not, he provided her with invaluable professional assistance – Jane showed talent, but so did many young actors, and it was no hindrance to have a famous name.

Fonda was a late starter but her progress was astonishingly swift. She was signed up by the Famous Artists agency and began working with prodigious success as a model. In July 1959 she was on the cover of *Vogue*. In assessing the stages of Fonda's extraordinary

Fonda with Roger Vadim: 'All I heard about him suggested he was vicious, sadistic and a maniac.'

career, it is sometimes difficult to assess the relative importance of luck, talent, shrewdness, determination and family connections. Being a successful photographic model has traditionally been one of the most effective stepping stones to a career as a Hollywood star and so it proved once more. The *Vogue* cover was brought to the attention of the stage and film director Joshua Logan by his wife. He was an old friend and collaborator of Henry Fonda's (he had directed and co-written *Mister Roberts*) and he knew that Jane was a student of Lee Strasberg.

He later claimed to have been doubtful of her commitment, 'as one always suspects newcomers who have successful parents'. Fonda's fellow students at the Actors Studio might have been grateful to be on the receiving end of such doubt. Logan signed her up for a five-picture, five-year contract for $10,000 a year and promptly cast her in the leading role in his next film, a light comedy called *Tall Story* (based on *The Homecoming Game*, a comic novel by the poet Howard Nemerov, brother of the photographer Diane Arbus). Fonda was entering the film industry in the dying days of the major studio control that her father had resentfully worked under. The year may have been 1960 but there were still remnants of the belief that stars had to conform to a rigid stereotype of physical attractiveness. One of the four original Warner Brothers, Jack, still ran the studio and he was critical of Fonda's looks, at least according to her own later, jaundiced recollection: 'She's got a good future if you dye her hair blonde, break her jaw and reshape it, and get her some silicone shots or falsies.' Her jaw remained intact, but she allowed her appearance to be remade, and she never forgot the humiliation she felt.

Fonda later claimed to have been painfully anxious about her first film role, and she had good reason. Good connections can give

Fonda's film debut, *Tall Story* (1960). That same year Anthony Perkins would appear in a less tender shower scene.

an actor an opportunity, but they aren't enough to sustain a career and there is particular pressure on an actor, such as Sofia Coppola in *The Godfather Part III*, who is thought to have benefited from nepotism. Fonda remembered having suffered from the suspicion of fellow actors and this is plausible enough. Roy Scheider, speaking as an admirer of Fonda's talent, recalled her early years in the business: 'I liked her passion. And her professionalism. You know, Jane worked for years as a silly ingenue on the stage in New York and, I mean, she was laughable at first. But she stayed with it and slowly, carefully, learned her craft.'

It must have seemed to struggling young actors who had been studying drama for years that this young upstart *ought* to have been laughable, but film is a very different medium from the stage and professional training counts for very little compared with a screen presence that is both indefinable and unmistakable. Jane Fonda had it from the beginning. *Tall Story* was a charming, minor comedy in which Fonda is a co-ed who falls in love with the college basketball star, played by Anthony Perkins. He was the leading young male star in Hollywood and Fonda was not outshone.

At this time there were two further tragedies connected, though more distantly, with the Fonda family. Margaret Sullavan, Henry Fonda's first wife and still a close friend of the family, had been suffering from depression caused by worsening deafness. At the beginning of 1960 she committed suicide. Later in the year her daughter, Bridget Hayward, who had a history of mental illness, killed herself also. The second death in particular devastated Peter Fonda, who had been in love with Bridget (and was to name his daughter after her). But whatever they suggested about the milieu from which Jane had emerged, she was now a grown-up

Jane Fonda and her co-stars in *Period of Adjustment*, Tony Franciosa and Jim Hutton, demonstrate the meaning of the phrase 'clean cut'.

With Anthony Perkins on the set of *Tall Story*.

with a degree of confidence that came from having a promising career of her own.

Jane had a series of relationships with fellow actors or students, most notably James Franciscus, who would later have a successful career in TV drama, and an unstable young actor, Timmy Everett. These were all painless enough (at least for her; when she broke off with Everett, he attempted a theatrical – and ineffectual – suicide in front of her). But her relationship with an associate of Strasberg called Andreas Voutsinas was more serious and revealing about Fonda's attraction to men who could offer her guidance. He was not a major talent but there was something of the guru about him, and during their affair he began to exercise an influence over her work. Anxiety about her career was scarcely necessary. She appeared in two Broadway plays and while Roy Scheider may have been laughing somewhere, critics were starting to hail her as one of the more talented actresses of her generation.

She was starring in major films as well – pictures directed by Edward Dmytryk, George Cukor and George Roy Hill – and the degree of her popularity was shown not least in the willingness of producers to tolerate the presence of Voutsinas on set, counselling Fonda on her performances. Under the terms of her contract with Joshua Logan, he would take any fees she earned while continuing to pay her $10,000 a year. After two years of this it was clear that he had much the better of the deal and Fonda paid him $250,000 to release her. It was a remarkable expression of self-confidence, and it was entirely justified. She earned the money back from her next role, in *Period of Adjustment*, another competent minor comedy, based on a play by Tennessee Williams. She was now one of the most successful young female stars, either on stage or on screen, and so she was duly named 'Miss Army Recruiting of 1962'. She was, it can safely be assumed, the first 'Miss Army Recruiting' actually to call on US servicemen to desert, but that would be ten years later, and in another country.

The sixties took a long time to arrive in the American cinema. The best of the old studio system – its sheer professionalism, its resources, its skill with such genres as musicals and thrillers – had been lost, but what remained in the ruins was not a new generation but what seemed like old men making films about a world they didn't understand. Jane Fonda's first three films were all directed by men of her father's generation (*Tall Story*, supposedly a 'youth picture', was written by one of the writers of *Casablanca*). Television was superseding the cinema in strictly commercial terms, and it was obvious that, creatively at least, European cinema was now more vibrant. Going to Europe had once been the last option of ageing or failing Hollywood stars who could no longer get big parts at home, or those who wanted to benefit from a tax break which allowed earning abroad to be untaxed (Gene Kelly's career never recovered from his attempt to benefit from this by making three quick films in Europe), or those who were black-listed in the McCarthy era. Now artistic ambition might be a motive as well. Jean Seberg, an actress of Fonda's age who had been contemptuously dismissed by critics after the debacle of her debut in Otto Preminger's *Saint Joan*, remade her reputation in 1959 by starring in Jean-Luc Godard's seminal New Wave film *Breathless*.

Fonda was already starting to speak to friends of being trapped by the limitations of American film and theatre. Her first European film was not, however, an assertion of independence. American studios had also started to feel that there were commercial opportunities in Europe and MGM sent Fonda to France to star with the new French star Alain Delon in *Les Félins* (*Joy House*) a film written and directed by René Clément. He must have seemed a safe choice. Not only was he a distinguished French director, but he had proven skill in working with English-speaking actors. And the story, about a playboy criminal on the run who holes up in a strange mansion presided over by two American women, must have seemed promisingly decadent. In fact, in retrospect it is obvious that Clément's best days – artistically, if not commercially – were behind him and the film was a poor affair. But Fonda enjoyed being back in France and began a liaison with Alain Delon, to the dismay of Voutsinas, who was still in semi-detached attendance. For her, it was like the old days, except that now she was a big star and instead of being summoned back to America by an angry father, she was questioned by lubricious, eager reporters. 'Alain is an extremely seductive man,' said Fonda coyly. 'And he's good to work with.'

She celebrated her twenty-fifth birthday in France and one of the guests at the party was Roger Vadim. He recalled being charmed by her French, despite its imperfections: 'In French she speaks in a much more colourful way and her voice is deep and nuanced. The lack of confidence that comes from seeking a word in a foreign language gives her a gentleness which is part of her character, but which, for reasons that I've never understood, she tries to hide.' Also, circumstances had changed since their last meeting. Vadim was unattached – or, rather, becoming detached from Catherine Deneuve – and Jane Fonda was famous. Early in the new year they spent the night together for the first time.

Fonda was sexually assertive and had had a large number of casual affairs. She was generally dominant in her relationships, and

Roger Vadim was less a father figure to Fonda than a naughty
cousin who freed her to have uninhibited adventures.

even where she placed herself in a subservient role, as with Voutsinas, it was out of a sense of what she needed from her partners. She took the initiative with Vadim and she later told him that she had been obsessed with him and wanted to rid herself of this inconvenient preoccupation by having sex with him. But Vadim outwitted her. When they got into bed together, he proved to be impotent and he stayed that way for three whole weeks. At the time it seemed to him like a curse, but it was typical of his idiosyncratic inert attractiveness.

Fonda had already been aware of Vadim's reputation, but then so were millions of people. As she later put it, 'all I heard about him suggested he was vicious, sadistic and a maniac'. According to legend, he had discovered Brigitte Bardot when she was a young and respectable teenager. He had corrupted her, married her, then put her into a sex film and watched uncaring as she had committed adultery with her co-star. Divorced from Bardot, he had turned his attention to manufacturing other blonde movie stars in her image.

In fact, to see Vadim as a cynical predator was to misread him completely. Far from being a bullying Svengali, he was more comparable to a male stick insect, who would turn his lovers into famous stars before they bit his head off and moved on. He sadly lacked the talent for making the stylish movies he aspired to, but he had a genius for finding and nurturing women. Even in his various works of autobiography, the reader can catch a whiff of the sweet passivity which encouraged his glamorous lovers to fulfil themselves. He seems to have been entirely lacking in machismo or in any need to compete with his lovers. He would calmly accompany them on their films or, if they were willing, use them in his own films. But somehow this would always do more for them than it did for him. He made them into new women, and generally the first thing the new woman wanted to do was to leave Roger Vadim.

It has frequently been said of Fonda that she has spent her life searching for father figures, but Vadim was more like a naughty cousin who freed her to have uninhibited adventures in Europe like an American heroine in an updated Henry James novel. Despite her success, she still lacked confidence both in her looks and her ability as an actress. Vadim encouraged her in both ways. Curiously, the sexual exploitation she later recalled so scathingly was a part of this process. She had already accepted the starring role in Vadim's next film, *La Ronde*. He tried to persuade her to appear nude in the film and she refused, but it was nice to be asked. *La Ronde* was a characteristic Vadim project. Adapted by the distinguished playwright Jean Anouilh, from Artur Schnitzler's drama of a series of linked sex acts (that Max Ophuls had so discreetly and elegantly filmed in 1950), it had culture and eroticism, and was botched in the execution.

One of Jane Fonda's most remarkable qualities was her ability to enter a new milieu, sense what was important and new about it, and absorb it. Nothing ever seems to have been wasted. As soon as she and Vadim were established as a couple she began learning French and embarked on a course of reading that he set out for her. She pushed herself into all the corners of Vadim's life. When she learned of his Russian ancestry, she arranged a long trip with him through the relatively more open Soviet Union of the Khrushchev thaw. When Annette Strøyberg was temporarily unable to look after Nathalie, her child by Vadim, Fonda became a devoted stepmother. And she showed her commitment to the relationship by buying a three-acre farm in the village of St-Ouen-Marchefroid, just west of Paris, and began restoring it herself.

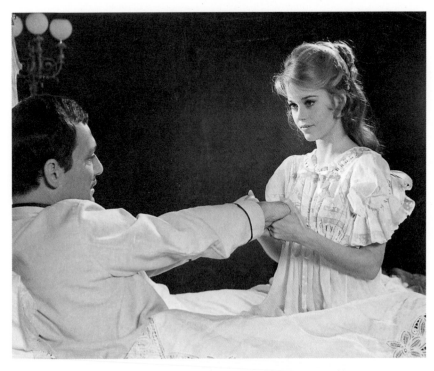

Fonda had an alternative European career in Vadim films
such as *La Ronde* (1964) with Maurice Ronet:
sophisticated, erotic, not much good.

A poster version of this still from *La Ronde* was displayed
in Times Square in New York City and led to
prosecutions for obscenity.

She also believed that Vadim could help her as an actress. She was well-enough trained, but the techniques she had learned from Strasberg and Voutsinas had taught her to be detailed and analytical. Vadim lacked most of the talents of his contemporaries in the French New Wave, but he shared their belief in spontaneity of performance. The fruits of this would be visible ten years later in her finest and most exposed performance, in *Klute*. As ever, it remained for other people to benefit from lessons taught, or at least encouraged, by Vadim.

She now felt settled in Europe, so when an offer arrived for her to star in a Western she was inclined to turn it down. But, by his own account at least, Vadim read the script for himself, and disagreed. 'I like *Cat Ballou*,' he says he said. 'The woman is courageous, but tender, modern and funny. It's just right for you at this stage of your career.'

He was right. Whatever else Jane Fonda gained from her life and career in Europe, she never made a film for Vadim that was as good as the films she was making in America at the same time. *Cat Ballou*, with its double-performance by Lee Marvin (for which he won an Oscar) and its captivating running commentary in song performed by Nat King Cole and Stubby Kaye is a delightful comedy Western and it is one of the finest examples of Jane Fonda as (in Pauline Kael's words) a 'naughty-innocent comedienne'. Fonda may have been right about her need to develop as an actress and as a person, but she also had the tendency (which she has retained) to be unfairly disparaging about a stage of her life when she felt she had moved beyond it. Films like *Period of Adjustment* and *The Chapman Report* (both made in 1962) are little seen now, so even admirers of Fonda's later work may be unaware of the skill and charm of those early, wide-eyed, skittish comic performances. Contrary to myth, Vadim made Fonda serious about herself, but, woefully lacking a sense of humour, he also encouraged a solemnity about herself and her roles.

Vadim accompanied Fonda back to Hollywood and was apparently content for the moment in his subordinate role. Reactions to Vadim were mixed. Even her father was grateful to him as the man who had seen off Andreas Voutsinas, and her friends and family were all won over by his modest style. But there was little enthusiasm for Jane's first film with Vadim and still less when the publicity campaign for the film (which failed utterly in America) featured a poster in Times Square in New York City showing Jane nude. This was subject to legal action for obscenity, and was hastily, crudely, patched over. (The Trades Descriptions Act might have been more appropriate, since Fonda didn't appear nude in the film itself.)

Fonda now entered on a double career. Back in Hollywood she continued her movie career as if she'd never been away, in films like *The Chase* (in which she acted with Marlon Brando) and *Hurry Sundown*. She interspersed these with leading roles in erotic films for Vadim in Europe. Her second film for him was *La Curée*, adapted from the Zola novel, in which she played a young woman who marries a wealthy older man (played by Michel Picoli) and then begins an affair with his son (played by the young British Royal Shakespeare Company actor, Peter McEnery).

This really was unprecedented. It wasn't all that unusual for Hollywood actors to make films in Europe, and it was becoming less so. A couple of years earlier, for example, Burt Lancaster followed his famous role as *The Birdman of Alcatraz* with an even more remarkable performance in Luchino Visconti's *The Leopard*.

Jane Fonda's 'commercial' films, such as the comedy western *Cat Ballou*, were actually better than her European 'art' films – and much more fun.

A heated moment from *Hurry Sundown* (1967). At least Fonda's Deep South accent was better than Michael Caine's.

But Jane Fonda was being two different kinds of actress. In Hollywood she was a major star, but not obviously different from other performers of her generation such as Natalie Wood or Joanne Woodward. In Europe she was a sex symbol created by Roger Vadim in the image of his first wife, Brigitte Bardot. And each acted as a comment on the other. In *Barefoot in the Park* (1967), a screen version of Neil Simon's Broadway comedy about young marrieds, Fonda gave another expert comic performance. But it seemed baffling that in 1967, the year of Haight-Ashbury, the summer of love, that Hollywood was still making films with jokes about honeymoons and young couples dealing with their in-laws. The moment where Fonda makes Robert Redford give her a proper goodbye kiss by threatening to take off her pyjama top as she stands on the landing outside their apartment could have been in a film ten years earlier (where it would have featured Doris Day and Rock Hudson). The scene is made even more absurd by the audience's awareness that when Fonda made films in Europe she didn't wear pyjamas at all.

Fonda's adoption of Brigitte Bardot's image was more interesting. Much of Bardot's appeal was founded on the notion, shamelessly encouraged by Vadim, that it was all just Bardot, that there was no barrier between the film and the life. She was the natural woman, a rebuke to the confected female icons of Hollywood. She embodied sex as a primal urge. Juliette in *And God Created Woman* acts on her impulses and it was well known that during the shooting of the film, Bardot had done the same with her co-star, Jean-Louis Trintignant. Vadim's relationship with his first wife was as paradoxical as that of his audience. The avid filmgoers thought they were seeing the real Bardot which transcended the particular

Back in America for *Barefoot in the Park* (1967)
with Robert Redford, Fonda was innocent and
wholesome once more.

In Europe, Fonda was the next Bardot. In America, she was
more like the next Doris Day.

role she happened to be playing. Vadim was married to Bardot, yet he was evidently more aroused by the image of Bardot, the Bardot on screen that was fantasised about by millions of people, than he was by the actual body that was available to him. Perhaps he was right. It was Dr Johnson who said to Boswell: 'Were it not for imagination, Sir, a man would be as happy in the arms of a chambermaid as of a Duchess.' Vadim is a man obsessed with flesh, yet who suspects uneasily that sex may be more an idea than an instinct. For Bardot sex was an appetite, for Vadim sex was looking at Bardot – preferably on screen.

When Fonda became, or impersonated, Bardot, the meaning changed. For Bardot it was a gratification of desire, for Fonda it was a career move, a demonstration of actorly virtuosity. Bardot's nudity represented the nakedness of the sexual impulse; for Fonda her naked body was a tool of her craft. Pauline Kael once wrote of Fonda that, as an actress, she had 'a special kind of smartness that takes the form of speed; she's always a little ahead of everybody'. When audiences saw *And God Created Woman* they felt they were seeing sex portrayed with a lack of artifice or ambiguity that was unprecedented in film history. The political and social implications were startling. What would a society be like that was based on self-fulfilment and gratification rather than duty? Answering that question was part of what the sixties was about. Jane Fonda could never be that simple, which is both her strength and limitation as an actress. She put it perfectly herself: 'I've always sort of played it close to the edge in my personal life, but careerwise I don't take risks.' This doesn't mean being cautious and attempting to lead the kind of orthodox Hollywood career that no longer existed. Actors who attempted that – people like George Peppard, Natalie Wood, Robert

Wagner – watched their careers fade away while mavericks like Warren Beatty, Dustin Hoffman and Jack Nicholson became the major stars. Fonda never seems to have taken a part casually, or without responsibility. She gives herself to a role, but she has never given herself to a director.

In the middle of all this, on 15 August 1965, when Jane was twenty-seven, she married Vadim in Las Vegas on an impulse. She signed the register as Lady Jane Seymour Brokaw Fonda, an assembly of her childhood nickname, mother's name and father's name, as if at the moment of her marriage all her family conflicts could be resolved. In fact, it was merely another example of them. Henry Fonda learned of the ceremony when he read about it in his newspaper.

It was never to be a conventional marriage. Vadim loved his wife but he was quickly bored by monogamy. Years later, Fonda would force her by-then ex-husband to remove some of the details of their sexual habits from his memoirs, but they were widely publicised – and were not, it should be said, much different from the Hollywood norm, except in their lack of hypocrisy. It is wrong to describe Vadim as unfaithful or cheating because he professed no faith, except to the gratification of desire, and was entirely open about his sexual behaviour. He also involved his wife, who was willing enough, in his sexual social life. When he grew tired of his own sexual experimentation, he would bring partners home and encourage his wife in sexual escapades, there and elsewhere. In his own memoir, John Phillips (of The Mamas and the Papas) gives an account of visiting the Vadim-Fonda household in Malibu and Vadim offering him his wife as if she were an *amuse-gueule* (and then being joined by Vadim, Warren Beatty and Michelle Phillips).

Fonda reflects on her decision to reject the leading roles in
Bonnie and Clyde and *Rosemary's Baby* to make *Barbarella*.

Jane Fonda is *Barbarella* (1968). If only the movie had been
as amusing – and as well-designed – as the poster.

For the rich and beautiful of Hollywood in the post-Pill pre-Aids era, it must have seemed like a sexual Nirvana and there were fragmentary plans to capture the spirit of the times on film. Terry Southern wrote a very funny novel called *Blue Movie* about a farcical attempt by a Hollywood director to make a big-budget sex film. He knew what he was talking about because he was a major creative presence both in Europe and the United States. He is one of the faces in the crowd on the cover of *Sgt. Pepper's Lonely Hearts Club Band* and he was the original scriptwriter on projects by both Jane and Peter Fonda in the late sixties, *Barbarella* and *Easy Rider*.

European and American culture appeared to be growing closer together and it seemed as if Hollywood movies might finally benefit from the independent, freewheeling style previously associated with Europe. It is no coincidence that of the two films that Jane Fonda misguidedly turned down in order to make *Barbarella*, *Bonnie and Clyde* had first been offered to François Truffaut and *Rosemary's Baby* was the US debut of the Polish director, Roman Polanski.

Barbarella was Vadim's chance for success in the commercial American market. With *And God Created Woman* he had brought a new frank, overt sexuality into the French cinema. What if he could do the same thing for the American cinema? *Barbarella* seemed the perfect subject for its time, a parodic SF comic strip about female sexual pleasure. It would bring together sophisticated, elegant design, humour, and a message in favour of sex and against violence. Fonda at first rejected the idea, but once more Vadim persuaded her: 'I explained to Jane that cinema was evolving and that the time was approaching when science fiction and galactic-style comedies like *Barbarella* would be important.'

Behind the near gibberish of the script in the released version (eight screenwriters are credited), one can detect glimpses of what might have been, a sort of sexual space odyssey in the style, perhaps, of Terry Southern's cod-pornographic novel, *Candy*. But Vadim, apart from lacking any comic touch, also lacked the basic skills to manage a large-scale film and keep a grip of the narrative, the design, the music. The film is a shambles, but rather an innocent, likeable shambles. Pauline Kael found it disappointing after the expectations she had had of 'a film that would be good trashy, corrupt entertainment, for a change. *Barbarella* isn't good trash, but it's corrupt, all right, and that's something.'

She acclaimed Jane Fonda as 'more charming and fresh and bouncy than ever – the American girl triumphing by her innocence over a lewd comic-strip world of the future. She's the only comedienne I can think of who is sexiest when she is funniest.' Even as described by Vadim, the conditions of shooting were difficult for Fonda, who had to suffer considerable discomfort from the costumes and sets. But she plays Barbarella in all her childish carnal delight with total aplomb, and she had the courage and shrewdness to play the character straight. It is a triumph of character and technique over the sheer incompetence and chaos of her surroundings. It may be that she loathed the role but she plays it with a flamboyance and sexiness that give some sense of what the film could have been.

It was an extraordinary achievement for Jane Fonda to avoid making a complete fool of herself in *Barbarella* and even when she became a feminist activist, she retained conflicting feelings about it. After all, however pitiful the film might be in other respects, Vadim had a sense of female sexual autonomy. As Fonda herself would later observe, 'most of the pictures where I was dressed to the teeth

Despite her misgivings, as *Barbarella* Fonda did whatever
Vadim wanted – even *wore* whatever he wanted.

Jane Fonda in 1969 with baby Vanessa and a
varied display of leather goods.

and played a cute little ingenue were more exploitative than the ones with the nudity because they portrayed women as silly, as mindless, as motivated purely by sex in relation to men.'

With her clear sense of her own career, however, Fonda was becoming aware that she had nothing more to gain from her professional association with Vadim. Her marriage was another matter. She decided she wanted a child and became pregnant. On 28 September 1968 she had a daughter, and they called her Vanessa (after her friend Vanessa Redgrave). Like many people, Fonda felt changed by motherhood and she expressed it drastically: 'I wasted the first thirty-two years of my life.' For a Hollywood actress there wasn't much time.

Chapter Three

ACTING

The first role Fonda was offered after the birth of her daughter was as the bleak, ultimately suicidal, heroine in the screen version of Horace McCoy's *They Shoot Horses, Don't They?* There had been many previous attempts to film this grim little fable (first published in 1935). Vadim himself had had a go, back in France in the early fifties. In the disillusioned late sixties era of the Vietnam War, Richard Nixon in the White House and Ronald Reagan as Governor of California, it had found its time. It tells the story of a dance marathon held in Los Angeles during the Depression in the early 1930s. The competitors are a bunch of losers and failures and Gloria, the heroine of this dark tale, is distinguished not by her success but by her recognition of hopelessness. She so convinces her dancing partner, Robert, of this that when she asks him to shoot her, he does so – hence the title. The story is narrated by Robert while the judge is pronouncing the death sentence.

In an interview given at this time, she was clear-eyed about the balance that needed to be maintained between her personal

Jane Fonda's finest performance, as Bree Daniels – a prostitute and actress – in *Klute* (1971).

and her professional lives (expressing an attitude that would become more common and is now routine): 'I am against huge sacrifices like giving up a career either for husband or family because that can lead to resentment. So Vadim and children and my career should all be mixed together so that later I can't say: "If I hadn't given this part up, look where I'd be."' Fonda has often been accused by her detractors of being inconsistent, a chameleon, as if everybody's priorities didn't shift as they grow up and then grow old. What is characteristic of Fonda is the totality of her commitment once she has decided on what should be her priority. At the beginning of her relationship she had given herself over to building a home for them, at times with her own hands. When she thought it necessary for them to be together, she had turned down major film roles (the part of Lara in *Dr Zhivago* that Julie Christie accepted was another example).

Now she decided it was time for her to be serious about her career and her life needed to be adjusted to make room for it. The couple moved back to the United States, installing Vadim's elder daughter, Nathalie, in a boarding school in Switzerland. Vadim later recalled plaintively that he had been against the idea.

The role of Gloria was entirely different from anything Fonda had played before, a departure both from the comedic lightness of her Hollywood persona and the eroticism of the roles she had played for Vadim. She immediately reinforced the point by restoring her hair to its natural, dark colour. She absorbed herself into the role to a degree that was entirely new for her. Not only did she conduct intensive research into the period and dance for extended periods in order to get a feel for the physical demands, but she actually moved away from home so that she could stay in character –

Michael Sarrazin and Jane Fonda as the desperate marathon
dancers in *They Shoot Horses, Don't They?* (1969)

and costume – for the whole period of shooting. Previously she had been habitually polite to colleagues during the shooting of her films, but now she was more determined, and more cut off from her colleagues. She was also more willing to argue with the director. And for the first time in her career, the director was a man she was responsible for appointing.

In his memoirs Vadim expressed shock at Jane Fonda's acceptance of the producers' decision to dismiss the film's writer and original director, James Poe – who had both initiated the project and first suggested Fonda for the leading role – and replace him with the more obviously commercial Sydney Pollack: 'I couldn't understand that attitude coming from a woman who was so sensitive to social injustice, to the corrupting power of money and to the lack of humanity in Hollywood's moguls.' This bemusement may suggest some of the reasons for the differences in their film careers. It may be that during his career Vadim considered issues of personal integrity to be more important than his films, and if so he may be the better man for having done so. Certainly Vadim's films give the consistent impression of a man whose priorities were elsewhere. On the other hand, it is not clear that a concern for social justice should mean that people don't get fired from films. Hitherto, Jane Fonda had had little power, whether in Hollywood or Europe, and, partly for that reason, she had been dissatisfied with her work. One result of the collapse of the studio system was that successful actors became more powerful and one inevitable result of being powerful is having to make decisions that harm people.

They Shoot Horses, Don't They? is not a film without flaws. Horace McCoy's original story works partly because of the low-key style in which it is told and its relatively small scale. Pollack made the story even more baroque, the milieu more wildly corrupt and orgiastic, the symbolism about the corruptions of American capitalism more obtrusive. There is even a problem with Jane Fonda's performance, which derives from its extraordinary strength. This is a story of a woman defeated by circumstances, beaten down, to the extent that when she tells a man that she is better off dead, he thinks that he is doing the right thing by killing her. Fonda's performance is so strong that if you step back from the histrionic, unrelenting pace of the film, it is difficult to imagine her as a failure. Indeed, it may well have been Pollack's growing sense of Fonda's electric power that made him soup up the action to such a pitch.

The film's willed decadence might have been scarcely watchable without Fonda. The other actors are too absorbed into Pollack's scheme of misery to engage us, and the leading actor, Michael Sarrazin, was sadly incapable of making passivity compelling. His career was failing as Fonda's prospered, and this film shows why. But the film does work, and a lot of that comes from Fonda's performance. It still seems extraordinary today, but at the time, when Fonda's reputation, whether fairly or not, was partly as a fluffy comedienne, partly as a sex star, it came as a revelation. Perhaps because she had been ingratiating for so long, Fonda felt released to be irredeemably harsh. Also, whatever else the film is about, it is savage about the tradition of Hollywood, with its veneer of decency and family values and the political and sexual corruption beneath. Fonda's performance is authentically brutal, without the smallest edge of sentimentality.

She received considerable acclaim and a first Oscar nomination. Her performance was far better than any other of the nominees, but maybe the voters at the academy were a little alarmed by their

Jane Fonda in the 1970s: being a movie star was
now no longer enough.

surprise at her achievement – could that film star's daughter, an ex-blonde who had taken her clothes off, really be that good? – and the award went to Maggie Smith in *The Prime of Miss Jean Brodie*.

Nevertheless, her career had been transformed, and, after shooting had finished, as if to demonstrate it in an assertive gesture, she had her hair cut short: 'I always had a deep-rooted need to be a boy,' she commented. 'And now I am one.' This feeling in her own life coincided with a larger sense of sombre change – but then her private life always seemed in tune with developments elsewhere. As California had briefly been the symbolic centre of a movement based on love and peace, now it would also be the location for disenchantment, most notoriously with the murders committed by followers of Charles Manson and the violence and death at the concert given by the Rolling Stones at Altamont. Some people were damaged by drugs (though in fact the effects of drugs on the film community would be much more serious from the seventies onwards). Others, of whom Fonda was certainly one, simply became tired of the pursuit of pleasure.

After *They Shoot Horses, Don't They?* Fonda visited India, as so many of her contemporaries had done. Unlike most of them she came away inspired not by the spiritual power of eastern religion but repelled and enraged by the poverty. Her politicisation had already begun in France, influenced by radical friends of Vadim (though he determinedly removed himself from politics), and by being in France during the upheavals of 1968.

Yet for once, her brother found himself more powerfully connected to the zeitgeist than she was. Peter Fonda's career had been moderately successful in the sixties but it seemed all too obvious that he would never escape the shadow of his more famous and talented father and sister, and he drifted into the exploitation pictures made cheaply by Roger Corman, and achieved welcome notoriety and something of a cult reputation in the biker movie *The Wild Angels* (1966) and the drug movie *The Trip* (1967). (Both were immediately banned in Britain, which then as now took special precautions to protect its citizens from corrupting images.) He also acted (ineffectually) opposite his sister in a short film directed by Vadim in 1968.

To observers, particularly those with a traditional sense of movie making, it must have seemed as if he had destroyed any chance of the stardom in movies that he craved. To friends of Jane he must have seemed like an amiable hanger-on, a good-looking, long-haired, slightly wild troubadour. He hung out on the beach, mixed with musicians, strummed some guitar, took drugs, appeared in a few cheap movies. Then he made *Easy Rider*, one of the most commercially successful and influential films ever made, on a par with *The Birth of a Nation* and *Gone with the Wind*.

Peter Fonda would always have a tendency to babble incoherent ideas for films that nobody could understand and that could never be made. *Easy Rider* seemed no different. One day he was lying slightly stoned in a hotel room in Toronto, when he glanced at a still from *The Wild Angels* showing him and Bruce Dern on a motorbike. He had the image of two men riding on *two* motorbikes across America. It would be a hip modern Western, two outsiders riding across country in search of the good place. It would end tragically. That was it. He thought the only person sufficiently in tune with him to understand what he was getting at was Dennis Hopper, his ex-brother-in-law. It was Hopper who suggested that they should be travelling on the proceeds of money earned from a drug deal.

A defining image of the 1960s: Peter Fonda in *Easy Rider*
(1969). It briefly made Peter the most famous Fonda.

It seemed a diffuse, hopelessly unsaleable idea, especially because of the drugs, and the head of the company who had produced Fonda's previous two films turned it down for that reason alone.

But for once in Peter Fonda's life, everything came together and turned out right for him. He was put in touch with Bert Schneider, a wild and brilliant young producer who had got rich by inventing The Monkees and now wanted to get into the movies. He was radical, highly intelligent and also well connected in the industry. He arranged a deal with Columbia Studios in return for a tightly restricted budget.

Fonda and Hopper brought together an extraordinary collection of young talent for their project. Fonda hired Terry Southern (whom he'd met on the set of *Barbarella*) as screenwriter, and the film benefited hugely from his ear for idiomatic Southern dialogue and a sense of craftsmanship that gave shape to Fonda and Hopper's various ruminations around the theme of rebellion and repression at the hand of the straights. Fonda would benefit even more when Southern left the project, in despair at the disorganisation, and Fonda obtained his share of the profits. The cameraman was the brilliant Laszlo Kovacs, who managed to capture a sense of epic space with minuscule resources. And the crucial supporting role of George Hanson, the drunken radical lawyer, was superbly played by Jack Nicholson, then almost unknown as an actor, though he had written *The Trip*. And a professional editor removed some of Dennis Hopper's more extreme counter-cultural touches (such as showing the opening scene upside-down).

What, apart from the original idea, did Fonda contribute? Himself, mainly. Fonda put his own face and his psyche up on the screen, and there is no question that this contributed to the air of paranoid self-absorption that was at the heart of its attraction. Fonda had always been daunted by the image of his father, and for *Easy Rider* he was able to adopt it. His character, with the American flag on his gas tank and his helmet, gains all too obvious resonance from the connections in the audience's mind with Henry Fonda's emblematic idealists, Tom Joad, Abe Lincoln, Wyatt Earp and the conscientious jury member in *Twelve Angry Men*. His mother was there as well. In the New Orleans 'trip' sequence, Dennis Hopper cajoled Fonda into improvising about the agony he experienced when his mother killed herself. Fonda was at first appalled by what he had revealed, but he was easily persuaded to allow it to stand. After all, his relationship with his father, from childhood to middle age, consisted of trying to force an intimacy on him that he couldn't tolerate. The idea of the conflict between generations in *Easy Rider* certainly gains force from the public message from son to father that is Fonda's performance.

If only the film was better, if only Peter Fonda was a better actor. Bruce Dern, who had acted with him repeatedly (and would later act with Jane), once lost all patience: 'In *The Trip* I started to get fed up. I was fed up because Peter Fonda was a star and I wasn't. And Peter couldn't act. I'm sorry, man, he just can't act. He never bothered to sit and learn. He never studied. And he just kind of larked out. Now I don't begrudge the fact that he has talent. But he's not an actor, by any stretch of the imagination.' It was Peter Fonda's very impassivity that struck a chord with audiences. There had always been a complacency, an untouchability about Henry Fonda's saintly young men and Fonda assumed a similar guise for his emblematic biker.

The film was a huge box-office success and Peter Fonda owned 22 per cent of it. He was the representative of a generation. Posters of him on his stars-and-stripes bike were on bedroom walls around the world. Within a year he earned more money than Henry Fonda had earned in his entire career. Finally, if only briefly, he had got his father's attention.

There were obvious lessons for Jane Fonda in the astonishing success of her brother. It was the most graphic demonstration possible that Hollywood filmmaking had changed. Actors were now able to take control of films. They could deal with subversive material, they could be idiosyncratically, painfully personal, without censorship from executives or regulators and make contact with a huge audience. Fonda and Hopper had succeeded, where large studios, established filmmakers and Roger Vadim had failed, in putting the counter-culture on the big screen. There was only one constraint. The moneymen, the straights, the suits, the establishment would allow you to do what you want so long as you earned money for them. Peter Fonda and Dennis Hopper would discover that the great new freedom and power they had gained within the industry amounted to one more film each. When their respective follow-up films, Fonda's muddled but powerful Western *The Hired Hand* and Hopper's wild *The Last Movie* flopped at the box-office, they were both on the outside again. It took years for Hopper to work his way back into mainstream success, largely as an outstanding character actor in such films as *Blue Velvet*. Peter Fonda, haunted now by his own image as well as his father's, never looked like sustaining a serious Hollywood career. Jane Fonda was always distrustful of the single spectacular success: 'A career is like building a house,' she said. 'And you hope you'll never finish.'

She returned from India with a new determination that was to leave no part of her life untouched. She arrived as her performance

Jane Fonda in *Klute*. She would never again
reveal such vulnerability.

in *They Shoot Horses, Don't They?* was being acclaimed on all sides and she was immediately greeted with offers of film roles. She turned down the part in Mike Nichols' *Carnal Knowledge* that would eventually go to Ann-Margret, probably because it was only a supporting role. She may well also have seen that it was a return to the essentially passive, lighter persona of her films of the earlier sixties. Having escaped from these roles, it would have been perverse to return to them, even in an intelligent, critical spirit.

Alan J. Pakula offered her another role that seemed on the face of it to be even less promising. It was another supporting part, it was playing another victim, a prostitute who is harassed by a stalker. The very title, *Klute*, suggested that it was really about the detective, John Klute, who comes from a small town to the infernal big city in search of a man who has disappeared. Pakula offered her the role of Bree Daniels, a high-class call girl with whom the missing man had been associated. The role seemed even more peculiar as a response to her brother's success. Peter Fonda had succeeded by playing a character that was conceived to be a folk hero, the subject of easy adulation. Yet Jane was intrigued by the character and saw that she could encourage an identification from the viewer that would be of a more complex and critical kind. She was in a position to exercise more power, and the entire script and her role were substantially rewritten in order to take Bree to the centre of the film.

She also had other kinds of acting on her mind, the need to do something, to get involved in political action, and she stumbled on an opportunity within minutes of getting off the plane from India. She picked up a copy of the radical magazine, *Ramparts*. On its cover was a photograph of American Indians who had occupied the old prison island of Alcatraz in San Francisco bay. The article inside informed her about the atrocious conditions in which these people lived. She contacted the editors of *Ramparts*, Peter Collier and David Horovitz. She told Collier that she was returning to America from Europe and that she wanted to do something. Would he take her to Alcatraz to meet the protesters? He agreed.

Collier's encounter with Fonda was very brief, but he was devastated by it, so much so that it goaded him into writing an obsessed, horrified book about the Fonda family years later. He took her over to the island and they chatted but when they arrived she immediately left him and made contact with the activists: 'When I left the island later that day, she was off in their corner of the old prison exercise yard smoking dope and listening to their stories.' When she returned to the mainland, she sought out Collier again and he helped her to plan a sort of activists' tour of America, taking her to reservations, army bases and university campuses. After she had set off, she wrote him an enthusiastic letter: 'My head has been turned 90 degrees.' And she promised that when they next met, she would have plenty of stories to tell him. As Collier ruefully observed, that next meeting never occurred. Like so many others who had introduced Fonda to a new experience, new country, new culture, new people, Collier watched Fonda seize the opportunity with gusto, make more of it than he could and then leave him behind.

The same had happened to Susan Strasberg, who brought her into acting and into her father's acting class; to Joshua Logan, who had put her under contract; to Andreas Voutsinas, who had given her a self-belief. Now it was happening to Roger Vadim. He saw that his wife was drifting away from him, and he felt helpless, but not all that distressed, let alone angry: 'I'm in no way a masochist, but it is part of my nature to like ambiguous, complicated, unclear situations. It was a change from the routine of love. It wasn't as disagreeable as one might think.' He was unsurprised when, on Valentine's Day 1970, she told him that she wanted to separate. Vadim rented a house on the beach in Malibu and took most of the responsibility for their little daughter. Fonda became virtually a full-time political activist.

After Peter Collier, she found other mentors, such as the radical Fred Gardner, with whom she began an affair, and the left-wing lawyer, Mark Lane (author of *Rush to Judgment*, the first significant book to challenge the findings of the Warren Commission), who helped her become involved with an Indian protest in Seattle where she was arrested for trespassing. The radicalisation of Jane Fonda was a very public event and attracted all sorts of responses. She began to be monitored by the FBI, she was interviewed on television (she made a particularly disastrous appearance on the *Dick Cavett Show* where her ignorance about the historical background of many of her new convictions was embarrassingly evident), she spoke to audiences across America. She was a mobile revolutionary, as she said in a statement that was Gandhi-like in its austerity, shrewdness and flair for publicity: 'All I need is two pairs of jeans, two sweaters and an air ticket.' Meanwhile, she attached herself to new causes, such as the Black Panthers, the paramilitary revolutionary group, and the anti-Vietnam War movement. As ever, the beneficiaries of the huge attention had mixed feelings. Many activists, especially among the American Indians, felt that the specifics of their grievances were being obscured. Critics then and later were divided about whether to mock Fonda for using radical agitators for her own selfish purposes, or for being used by the

Fonda, always the centre of attention, protesting on behalf of
Native American Indians in Denver, Colorado in 1970.

agitators for their purposes. She was enraptured that these Indians, Panthers, GIs, 'my new friends', treated her 'as a person', though they were probably as star-struck as everybody else.

Her political career developed as quickly as her acting career had ten years earlier and continued during her political tour. 'I took off on that trip a liberal,' she observed, 'and I ended up a radical.' The repercussions from Fonda's political radicalism even involved her father, when she had meetings with the revolutionary, Angela Davis, in his New York city townhouse. Henry Fonda recalled a discussion they had on the terrace one evening: 'I said, "Jane, if I ever discover for a fact that you're a Communist or a true Communist sympathiser, I, your father, will be the first to turn you in."' Jane claimed not to recall this conversation and indeed the meaning of his threat to 'turn in' his daughter is not clear, since even at the height of McCarthyism in the fifties, membership of the Communist Party had not been a criminal offence. Nevertheless the signficance of the story for Henry Fonda, whether it really occurred or not, is obvious. A life-long liberal, he was not only an anti-communist on principle but had seen Hollywood careers ruined by imprudent political activism. It was his daughter, more than anybody else, who was about to show how the rules had changed.

Meanwhile, shooting began on *Klute*. It must have seemed to many of the film's technical crew that Fonda's priorities lay elsewhere. Pakula later admitted to worries about whether his star might lose her grip on the role. During the filming of *They Shoot Horses, Don't They?* Fonda had ostentatiously stayed in character, but between takes of *Klute* she was almost permanently on the phone co-ordinating the details of her increasingly complicated political activities. Yet this may not have been as much of a distraction as it seemed. The drama of Bree, and it is implied of all women, is that of having to maintain different levels of existence, being glamorous, businesslike, attracting men while attempting to control them.

Fonda took control of *Klute* and made it her own story, her analysis of the conflicts and different sides of her personality. The equation between acting and prostitution that the film makes is not in itself novel or interesting but is made so by the raw brilliance of Fonda's performance and the willingness of Pakula to go with it and give it the detailed attention it deserved. The real drama in *Klute* is not the humdrum thriller plot but the unsparing portrait of female powerlessness. The audition scenes in the film are horribly well done and give plausibility to what otherwise might be the glib notion that Bree feels exhilaration as well as self-loathing at her prostitution because it is a transaction that gives a certain control. And yet, as we are shown, this control is itself an illusion.

In later films, Jane Fonda would frequently show the progression from weakness to strength. What makes Bree her greatest performance, and one of the great performances of its time, is that the intelligence and self-delusion, the control and the powerlessness, are combined. One might also add that though this is, by far, the most naked, intimate performance she would ever give, it was also the one in which she disappeared most completely into a character. As a performance it wasn't just outstandingly accomplished, it seemed important. In a film like *Easy Rider*, radicalism seems little more than an affectation. *Klute* forces the viewer to reconsider the notion of women in the movies. Were not we, as viewers, complicit in the debased sexual power exercised by casting directors on our behalf and, for that matter, by patrons of prostitutes?

Jane Fonda in costume as Bree Daniels in *Klute*.

It could be argued, however, that, once again, Fonda's performance was too powerful for the film it happened to be in. She was a radical actress in the tired remnants of the thriller form. *Klute* bore too many traces of the earlier version that had been reworked for its female star. By this time Donald Sutherland was in love with Fonda, in fact having an affair with her, and this may be why he allowed himself to be turned into a numb bystander on the edge of what ought to have been *his* film. The raw, documentary-style sequences featuring Bree talking to her psychiatrist don't seem to be in the same movie as the lurid episodes with Roy Scheider as her ex-pimp and the contrived suspense scenes at the end, frighteningly effective though they are.

Fonda had given two triumphant performances in a row and the second had established her without any question as one of the finest film actresses of her time. Even after the first of them, Pauline Kael had expressed huge hopes for her future, writing that she 'stands a good chance of personifying American tensions and dominating our movies in the seventies as Bette Davis did in the thirties; if so, Gloria will be but one in a gallery of brilliant American characters.' Kael's hopes for Fonda were both fulfilled more fully than she could have expected and disappointingly dashed. Jane Fonda would come to personify American tensions in both the seventies and the eighties, and maybe the nineties as well. But the 'gallery of brilliant American characters' never materialised. In retrospect, the fascinating tension of her performance as Bree came not because it was a culmination but rather because it caught her at the moment of transition, and not just that, but of Fonda observing her own transition. She was consciously leaving behind what she saw (unjustly) as the empty professionalism of her early years. The logical result of the internal debate that is so vividly externalised in *Klute* was a determination to secure genuine power over her work. She succeeded triumphantly, but there was a price to pay. The crisis is more artistically compelling than the resolution.

When shooting finished on *Klute* in October 1970, Fonda went back on the road. Flying into Cleveland, Ohio, after a visit to Canada, she was stopped by customs officers. They found some pills in her possession, confiscated her address book (which was duly copied by the FBI), and arrested her. She was roughly treated and when she pushed back was charged with assault, and illicitly carrying a supply of controlled drugs, and was put into a cell for ten hours. It was obviously a crude attempt at harassment of a supposed subversive. The charges were quietly dropped six months later after a federal laboratory test showed that the alleged illegal drugs were in fact vitamins.

In February 1971 Fonda and a group of other performers, writers and directors (including Donald Sutherland, Mike Nichols, Peter Boyle, the cartoonist Jules Feiffer and the comedian Dick Gregory) announced their formation of FTA, which stood for Fuck the Army or sometimes, for the benefit of the press, Free the Army. It was a challenge to the entertainment that had traditionally been provided for the forces by figures like Bob Hope and, for that matter, Henry Fonda. It was an anti-war comedy show that would be performed in venues close to army bases.

Fonda robustly rebutted any suggestion that she might be damaging her career: 'I keep calling my agents and asking if there is any effect and there isn't. As long as someone can make a buck off me they're gonna do it. And as long as I can go into Hollywood and make a movie and make a lot of money which I can use to support the struggles I'm involved with, I will.' The FTA show was feeble, but attracted large audiences of GIs grateful for any relief from the boredom of life on base. FBI investigations attempted to secure evidence against Fonda, but couldn't even prove that she had been encouraging soldiers to desert. On the other hand, the FBI might have been interested that on a visit to Paris Fonda had already had a secret meeting with North Vietnam's negotiator at the peace talks. It hardly mattered. Within eighteen months everybody would know about it.

The FTA team also made a film together, the amusing, likeably shambolic *Steelyard Blues*, about a collection of misfits who try to build an aeroplane. Fonda now seemed determined to demonstrate a different attitude on the set of every film she made. On *They Shoot Horses, Don't They?* she had been the dedicated Method actor; on *Klute* she was the full-time political activist for whom being a film star was a distraction; on *Steelyard Blues* her feminism became overt for the first time. For anybody who had seen *Klute* and digested its message about the treatment of the domination of women by men in the workplace, it shouldn't have come as a surprise. Interviewed by the *New York Times*, she spoke of her new sense of the everyday, casual insensitivity with which men treat women: 'Like when a woman starts telling a story, the men interrupt and finish it because they assume that no one will really understand or find amusing or interesting the way the woman tells it. And so the man has to take over and tell it his own way.' This has been quoted against Fonda has a sign of her blinkered feminism, but it might be said in response that her detractors mocked her claims that she was under FBI surveillance until the files were opened in the eighties and she was shown to be correct. Likewise, Fonda's description of men

Jane Fonda was at her funniest, most charming and
most underrated in *Steelyard Blues* (1972).

excluding women from conversations has been abundantly confirmed by later research conducted by linguists (Deborah Tannen's books on the subject have become bestsellers).

In this respect, radical activists were little different from other organisations, except that women weren't even treated with the chivalry that conservatives accorded them. Radical men did the talking and made policy, radical women licked envelopes, cooked and were supposed to be sexually available. When Fonda and a group of female associates tried to assert their authority with FTA, men like Fred Gardner and the singer Country Joe Macdonald (who denounced her as 'totalitarian and simple minded') left, and the organisation largely fell apart.

What sort of films should a radical actress make? *Steelyard Blues* had virtually been the work of a collective. Fonda had disliked the experience and the film was a commercial flop. In January 1972 Fonda went back to France to make a film very different from anything she had done with Vadim. Jean-Luc Godard had been one of the most brilliant directors of the French New Wave, but by the late sixties he had rejected what he considered to be corrupt bourgeois movie-making in favour of an overtly Marxist cinema devoted to political action. Fonda was to star with Yves Montand in *Tout va bien*, the story of an apolitical American journalist (played by Fonda) who is politicised by visiting the scene of a French strike. Once more, Fonda loathed working on the film. 'Godard hates people,' she later said, 'especially women.' (This judgment, incidentally, is endorsed even by Godard's admirers, such as David Thomson, who noted his 'pinched, cynical and misogynist aura'.)

It's mostly a dull, foolish film, but Fonda herself is wonderfully game in it. Actors frequently have a lost, hunted look when

Fonda with Donald Sutherland, her co-star in *Steelyard Blues* and, briefly, her lover.

Fonda, bespectacled and serious, with Yves Montand in Jean-Luc Godard's *Tout Va Bien* (1972).

they find themselves in a film they dislike, but Jane Fonda has never been like that. In *Tout va bien,* she acts with total conviction and is very fine in the film's one exciting scene, a long camera movement following Fonda's progress in a single take along a line of check-out tills in a supermarket. More than this, Peter Collier has shrewdly observed that the film had a crucial influence on the future of Fonda's films back in the United States. Godard's story, of the progress from apolitical innocence to principled commitment, would be the basic pattern that she would use repeatedly for the rest of the decade. Whether it was a good lesson to learn is another matter, though the commercial success of the result was undeniable.

While she was in Paris, she had secret talks once more with representatives from North Vietnam. The purpose was to fulfil an ambition she had held ever since she had become politicised a couple of years earlier: to visit Hanoi, the capital of North Vietnam. On her return to Los Angeles, she addressed an anti-war meeting at the Embassy Theatre. After the event was over, Tom Hayden came up on stage and introduced himself to her. They had met briefly before and Fonda was well aware of his reputation. He was a radical intellectual, a gifted organiser and a formidable influence on the counter-culture. Even as a student he had organised demonstrations against racial segregation, but he rose to national prominence as one of the organisers of the demonstrations that disrupted the Democratic National Convention in Chicago in 1968. As a result of this Hayden was subpoenaed by the House Committee on Un-American Activities. This was the committee which had played a notorious role in Hollywood history by subpoenaing actors, writers and directors and compelling them to name people they knew to be members of the Communist Party. Those who refused to collaborate with the committee were blacklisted by the movie industry and unable to work (at least under their own names). The committee gained much of the power from the fear that the Hollywood community had of it, particularly of the affect it might have on their careers. Tom Hayden and his colleagues gave the final *coup de grâce* to the committee by treating it with contempt. They were happy to discuss their revolutionary politics and utterly heedless of anything the committee might do to them. It is almost comic to contrast the cowed attitude of the witnesses in the post-war decade with exchanges such as the following, between Hayden and the committee's special counsel, Frank Conley:

MR CONLEY: *Mr Hayden, is it your present aim to seek the destruction of the present American democratic system?*
MR HAYDEN: *That is a joke.*
MR CONLEY: *I am asking you, sir.*
MR HAYDEN: *Well I don't believe the present American democratic system exists.*

Jane Fonda and Tom Hayden had more in common than was immediately obvious. Both were paradoxical rebels who were also drawn to the mainstream. Even in his days as a revolutionary, Tom Hayden was torn between wanting to get rid of the President and wanting to *be* the President. What *was* immediately obvious was that they could do a lot for each other. Like Fonda, Tom Hayden was under FBI surveillance, but his power was far less than it seemed. The revolutionary left had shown its traditional capacity to splinter into groups who spent most of their time fighting each other while capitalism and imperialism were left to their own devices. After one such conflict, Hayden himself had actually been expelled from a Berkeley commune he had helped form and was now without any power base. An association with Fonda was an obvious way back into politics, preferably with a higher profile.

Hayden also had a lot to offer Fonda. He had already visited Hanoi (back in 1965) and he had the contacts to help in a very risky and provocative act. Also he was an intellectual and a strategist, and could give a theoretical basis to Fonda's radical impulses. They quickly became lovers, but Fonda recalled that even before that she had been sure that this was the man she would marry.

Everybody expected Fonda to win the Academy Award for *Klute*. One of the few Academy members not to vote for her was her own father, as he revealed in his memoirs. His reason was that he didn't 'believe in that kind of competition', a distrust often felt for Academy Awards by those who have failed to win one. The principal tension of the evening was what she might say when receiving the award. Would she harangue the audience about Vietnam, American Indians, Black Panthers, women's rights? Even at the height of her radical involvement, she retained – most of the time – a wary tactical sense. Her acceptance speech was one of her finest performances, cool and authoritative: 'There's a lot I could say tonight, but this isn't the time or the place. So I'll just say "Thank You".' There was an audible gasp of gratitude from the audience and organisers, for whom embarrassment was the worst possible sin.

But those who believed Jane Fonda had been tamed by success and would now settle down to be a good, rich little actress were about to be disabused.

Chapter Four

COMING HOME

T om Hayden's first strategic advice to Jane Fonda proved to be disastrous. It was to doom his ambitions for success in the political mainstream right from the beginning. He decided that she was dissipating her energy and her effectiveness by campaigning on too many fronts. Instead, the two of them would concentrate their efforts on the campaign against American intervention in Vietnam and as the first big gesture the two of them would visit Hanoi.

Hayden rightly judged that such a trip by the Oscar-winning actress would be of huge symbolic value and would attract a great deal of attention. Fonda could be naïve over details of policy but nobody could doubt her flair for political gestures. It was perfectly possible to oppose the Vietnam War without defending the communist Vietcong whose brutality towards those who resisted them was

Jane Fonda in 1979, happily clutching her Academy Award for *Coming Home*.

systematic and remorseless. But in practice many American protesters, including Fonda and Hayden, represented the North Vietnamese as blameless victims of US imperialism. Years earlier Hayden had compared the Vietcong with the American revolutionaries, and when Fonda arrived in Hanoi, on an Aeroflot flight from Paris on 8 July 1972, it was in the belief that she was visiting a peace-loving nation, provoked reluctantly into defending its homeland by the American military machine.

During her fortnight in North Vietnam, Fonda displayed her uncanny skill at supplying soundbites and photo-opportunities. She threw herself into the tour with her characteristic flamboyance and commitment. Her histrionic, theatrical genius found a perfect setting. Whatever role Jane Fonda assumed, she would try to play it better than anyone had ever played it before. In Hanoi she gave the greatest and most memorable performance of any anti-Vietnam War protester. She visited bombed schools and hospitals. She was photographed standing by an anti-aircraft gun and applauding the gunners, and then looking through the gun-sight herself. She recorded speeches for Radio Hanoi which were broadcast to US servicemen and which described their actions as those of war criminals, 'and in the past in Germany and Japan, men who were guilty of these kinds of crimes were tried and executed.'

Finally, she appeared at a press conference in Hanoi with American prisoners of war who joined her in demanding that the United States forces leave Vietnam. There is no doubt that the prisoners spoke as they did because they had been tortured, or threatened with torture, and that others who refused to appear with her were severely punished. (The allegation that one prisoner who refused was executed is almost certainly untrue.)

14 July 1972: Fonda visits the troops – the North Vietnamese
troops. She would never be forgiven.

19 January 1973: Fonda and Tom Hayden at home. Peter
brought his guitar. Vietnamese folk songs were sung.

The quintessential Jane Fonda of the 1970s:
a microphone, a crowd and a cause.

At least a partial case for Fonda's trip to North Vietnam can still be made. It was a courageous and, on its own terms, a principled gesture, and some of what she said was right. We now know that American political leaders had concluded years earlier that the Vietcong could not be defeated militarily yet had kept American troops in Vietnam because they could think of no politically acceptable way of getting them out. American GIs on the ground might have argued with Fonda about the moral status of their opponents but by 1972 most of them were all too convinced of the hopelessness of the war they were fighting. They didn't need Jane Fonda to destroy their morale; they could manage that for themselves. It was a murky conflict in which one President announced a decrease in troop numbers while he was increasing them and his successor authorised secret bombings of a neutral country as a tactic in helping the peace talks' progress. Some of the beliefs of the anti-war protesters were false, but their conviction that the war had to be ended as soon as possible on almost any terms can scarcely be said to have been refuted by actual events.

Yet is difficult to avoid the judgement that Jane Fonda's Hanoi visit was appallingly and culpably misguided. Her gleeful pose by the Vietcong anti-aircraft gun showed a woman whose adroitness at symbolic protest outstripped adequate comprehension of the meaning of what she was doing. Her appearance with American prisoners of war exposed what was at best a disgraceful naïvety (Tom Hayden's participation in the charade might well be judged more harshly). Even in retrospect, it is difficult to see how she and Hayden thought it sensible to broadcast on Radio Hanoi, especially because of the dark tradition of such incitements to disaffection in the Second World War. But the fact that it seemed justified does reveal the depth of the divisions in American society during these years. After all, the police, the National Guard, the army, were all parts of the repressive forces that had beaten demonstrators in Chicago and killed students at Kent State University. Weren't they the enemy rather than the Vietcong? Reflections of this kind doubtless prevented Fonda and Hayden from considering what the characteristic Vietcong response was to far milder protests by their opponents in South Vietnam.

Finally, it cannot be said that Fonda's visit – ill-judged, irresponsible, and wrong-headed though it may have been – was of any wide significance. After Somalia and Bosnia, we have less difficulty in concluding that the American intervention in Vietnam failed because it couldn't have succeeded, and that the war ended when it did because the American will to continue it collapsed.

It is scarcely surprising that Fonda's actions, publicised around the world, caused fury back home and provoked immediate calls for legal action. Yet if the Nixon administration was the instrument of repression that Fonda and Hayden had claimed, it was a remarkably ineffectual one. The State Department immediately issued a public statement rebuking her for her broadcasts, but in almost comically mild tones: 'It is always distressing to find American citizens, who benefit from the protection and assistance of this Government, lending their voice in any way to governments such as the Democratic Republic of Vietnam – distressing indeed.' At this time President Nixon began to compile lists of his enemies and memoranda were prepared targeting them for harassment, but specific measures failed repeatedly. A tactic frequently employed during the fifties against the so-called threats to national security posed by figures like Leonard Bernstein, Arthur Miller and Paul Robeson had been to confiscate their passports in order to stop them travelling abroad. It might have been thought that this sanction could have been workable as a means of preventing travel to a country with which the United States was, effectively, at war. The State Department had suspended the passports of people travelling to North Vietnam, but these actions were successfully challenged in the courts and large numbers of Americans visited Hanoi.

The Justice Department launched an investigation into Fonda's visit, but this too proved to be a fiasco when five secret FBI memoranda were leaked showing that American bank officials had illegally passed on financial information about Fonda to the Bureau. President Nixon reportedly had plans to press ahead with an indictment, but the Watergate scandal and his resignation put an end to that. Fonda delightedly reported that the men who had been pursuing her were now in prison. But alone of all her actions during her period of activism, her Hanoi visit would never be forgotten. Ironically, the long-term harm that the trip caused was to Fonda and Hayden themselves.

When they returned to the United States the couple decided to have a child and it was conceived during a nationwide speaking tour in support of George McGovern. (That two of his most prominent supporters were facing possible indictments for treason was symptomatic of the McGovern presidential campaign, and he went down to the heaviest defeat in American electoral history.)

It was starting to seem as if Fonda's optimism about the effect that her activism would have on her career had been misplaced. She was now almost universally regarded as the finest screen actress of her time, but the major studios were wary of offering major roles to a woman who was so hated by a substantial portion of their audience.

So, for want of anything better and at a small fraction of her normal fee ($35,000 plus 15 per cent of the profits, which proved to be non-existent), Fonda accepted the role of Nora in a screen version of Ibsen's great play, *A Doll's House*, which was to be shot in Norway. It was adapted by the British playwright David Mercer, and directed by Joseph Losey.

This film version of a feminist masterpiece, adapted by a radical playwright and directed by a left-wing director who had fled the blacklist, should have been a meeting of minds but was torn by acrimony from beginning to end. Fonda's assistant, Nancy Dowd, insisted on changes to Mercer's script, mainly to make it more faithful to the original. Fonda and her co-star Delphine Seyrig felt themselves intimidated by the entirely male production team, and their hostility was returned by the traditionally sexist camera crew who responded by deliberately trying to intimidate the actresses. The resulting film was, though competent enough, a financial failure. Probably it would have flopped anyway, but not only was there a rival film version released simultaneously (starring Claire Bloom), but the principal publicity for the Fonda version consisted of expressions of mutual antagonism by Losey and Fonda in the press. As Fonda told one journalist: 'The strangest thing happened: I found I had to become Nora with Losey, bat my eyelashes, and make it seem as though it was his idea. A perfectly normal, well-disciplined actress who had some ideas about the play, that he couldn't handle. And this from a man who calls himself a progressive and a Marxist.'

Her experience since *Klute* suggested that it was no longer feasible for her to work as an actress for hire in the traditional way. She was considered a commercial risk and she was no longer willing

Fonda as Nora in Joseph Losey's *A Doll's House*.
She was unhappy on-screen and off.

to be a passive tool in the hands of a male director (of the thirty-eight films Jane Fonda has made in her career, only one, the documentary record of the FTA show, has been directed by a woman). She would have to find another way.

On 16 January 1973 she obtained a quick divorce from Roger Vadim and three days later she married Tom Hayden at her house in Laurel Canyon. This time Henry Fonda was not only informed but present, with his own fifth and final wife, Shirlee. The ceremony diverged from that outlined in the Common Prayer Book, most obviously when the priest asked the bride: 'Will you, Jane, marry Tom, and will you try in the marriage to grow together, to be honest, to share responsibility for your children, and to maintain a sense of humour?' The last question was Fonda's own self-mockery at her reputation for humourlessness. The celebrations continued with Irish jigs and Vietnamese folk songs. The Vietnamese theme was continued when Fonda gave birth to a son on Independence Day and he was named Troi O'Donovan Garrity – after Nguyen van Troi, who had tried to assassinate the Secretary of Defense Robert McNamara in the mid-sixties. Later, when Tom Hayden was trying to establish a reputation as a moderate who no longer applauded the assassination of American government officials, the name was quietly changed to Troy.

The signing of the peace treaty between the United States and North Vietnam, for which the couple had been campaigning, brought them unexpected problems in the shape of returning prisoners of war, some of whom denounced her Hanoi visit. She retaliated, describing them as hypocrites and liars. 'History will judge them severely,' she rashly predicted. Speaking to an audience at the University of California at Los Angeles, she went much further:

'Never in the history of the United States have POWs come home looking like football players. These war criminals are being made heroes. These football players are no more heroes than Custer was. They're military careerists and professional killers.'

Fonda's position, both as an effective polemicist and as an actress, now seemed precarious, and it was unclear whether she had the capacity, or indeed the will, to do anything about it. When, in 1974, Fonda and Hayden paid $45,000 for an ordinary house in a run-down part of Santa Monica, this was partly a conscious rejection of the Hollywood lifestyle but also a reflection that she didn't have very much money. If her political activities now seemed restricted to futile statements of self-defence that only damaged her reputation further, then her film career was hardly looking more promising. She formed a film company, provocatively titled Indochina Peace Campaign, with Bruce Gilbert, a man she had got to know when he worked at the co-operative kindergarten where she had sent her daughter Vanessa. But he wasn't just a drop-out. He was a lawyer who had worked on the defence of Daniel Ellsberg, the psychiatrist who became world famous for leaking the 'Pentagon Papers' to the *New York Times*. He had a knowledge of the film world and a belief that radical films could be made within the commercial system. The company got off to an unpromising start, however, with a sixty-minute agit-prop documentary about Vietnam called *Introduction to the Enemy*. Fonda then accepted one of the leading roles (opposite Elizabeth Taylor) in *The Blue Bird*, to be shot in the Soviet Union and directed by the Hollywood veteran George Cukor. It involved spending six weeks in Leningrad early in 1975 for what was only a supporting role, which became even smaller when it was heavily cut in the editing. Fonda would probably have been happier if she had been cut out altogether, since this attempt at a children's fantasy and an expression of *détente* between the American and Soviet film industries is now remembered only as one of the great disasters of film history, a misfired, barely intelligible movie that almost nobody ever saw.

It was a time when Fonda and Hayden had to consider whether they could salvage their respective careers. Hayden had never held elected office. Fonda hadn't acted in a hit film for almost five years. What were they to do?

With Fonda's support, Hayden decided to challenge the sitting California senator, John Tunney, for the Democratic nomination. Fonda's support was more than just emotional. There were strict rules about campaign contributions in California, but there were no restrictions on the money you could give to your own campaign. Fonda contributed half a million dollars, an extraordinary amount for what was only a prelude to the real election, especially as Hayden had no hope of winning. But he gained an impressive 37 per cent of the vote and showed that he could be a credible candidate. Together, Hayden and Fonda founded the Campaign for Economic Democracy, which would be the basis of Hayden's own political career, and would support a host of radical causes, ranging from green protest groups to non-union workers. It was a shrewd recognition that the future of radical politics lay not in the mobilisation of the proletariat, but in targeted single issues, often conducted on a local level. It was an effective way of covering the range of their interests. The question was whether it could be effective in getting Hayden elected to a significant political office.

As for herself, Fonda and IPC initiated what would be the most single-mindedly commercial project of her entire career, and it reflected a shift of emphasis. Fonda and Bruce Gilbert agreed that

Julia (1977): a new radical, Jane Fonda plays an old radical,
Lillian Hellman. Hellman was rightly delighted.

Fonda in *Julia* with her old friend, Vanessa Redgrave, whose luminous performance won her a Best Supporting Actress Oscar.

Jon Voight as the paraplegic Vietnam veteran and Jane Fonda as the sexually and politically unfulfilled army wife both won Oscars for *Coming Home.*

the most effective way of getting their political message across would be in the context of traditional forms, rather than polemical documentaries that would only be seen by audiences who agreed with them already. *Fun with Dick and Jane* consciously returned Fonda to the world of *Barefoot in the Park* and, for that matter, *Period of Adjustment* and *Tall Story*, but in a satirical style. It's a crude fable about the children's characters, Dick and Jane, grown up and living in affluence. When Dick (played by George Segal) is fired, they can only maintain their lifestyle by turning to crime. It improves their marriage and even results in Dick getting his job again. The film's message about the evils of consumerism was lamentably crude, the direction by Ted Kotcheff was barely competent, but Fonda herself came out of the film well. She was now approaching forty and it suggested promisingly that she could have a radiant middle age.

The film was a hit. In the wake of its success, Fonda secured the major role of Lillian Hellman in Fred Zinneman's film version of her 'memoir' *Julia* (it has since been established that the story is a mixture of plagiarism and fiction) and she persuaded the producer to hire Vanessa Redgrave to play the name part. As the producer later commented, 'It was perfect symmetry. The two most famous left-wing women of the seventies playing two left-wing women of the thirties. Of course, the fact that Jane and Vanessa were both terrific actresses didn't hurt, either. Not to mention that they both agreed to work cheap.'

Julia is in many ways an absurd film, but it is beautifully made and acted, especially by Vanessa Redgrave (who won the Best Supporting Actress Oscar), and Fonda looks glorious in it. During the shooting of the film Fonda showed good judgement by distancing herself from Redgrave's political extremism and she showed prudence in her performance also. She may well have decided that audiences knowing her reputation would expect stridency from her and be repelled by it. Some stridency might have been appropriate in portraying Lillian Hellman, one of the toughest and most self-suffi-cient of writers, but, in keeping with the glowing, lyrical style of the film, she played her as a tentative, eager ingenue, under the shadow both of her friend, Julia, and her lover, Dashiell Hammett (crustily impersonated by Jason Robards who won the Best Supporting Actor Oscar). This would be essentially the character she would play in her next eight films, almost all of which would be major hits, the inno-cent vulnerable woman changed by force of circumstances and the inevitability of events into a forceful radical not unlike Jane Fonda.

In little more than a year, Fonda had retrieved her reputation as a star. She was the first actress in film history to turn her career around at the age of forty. Now she could use her new power to make a film about an issue that was at the heart of her political beliefs. Some years earlier Fonda had had the idea of basing a story on the experiences of Ron Kovic, the paraplegic Vietnam veteran who had become an anti-war activist. When Kovic signed a deal else-where (which would, after many years, result in Oliver Stone's *Born on the Fourth of July*), she and her associate Nancy Dowd pressed on with a similar scenario about the wife of a soldier away in Vietnam who is changed by the experience of working in a veterans hospital. Crucially, the film would not be presented as a story of politicisation but of awakening love and sexuality. It would be about her love affair with a wheelchair-bound veteran and would feature what had previ-ously been a screen taboo, sex with a disabled man.

There was a lengthy process of rewriting and then further complications in casting the role of Sally's disabled lover. Jack

Nicholson, Al Pacino and Sylvester Stallone all turned down the role so, in desperation, Jon Voight, who was to play the husband, switched roles and was replaced by Bruce Dern. The finished film, *Coming Home*, directed by Hal Ashby, was certainly impressively honest, indeed groundbreaking, in its portrayal of disability, and nobody could question that Fonda had subordinated her political views to the love story. In fact, she had subordinated them to such a degree that, perhaps because of the amount of rewriting and the time that the project had been worked over, it was difficult to see what the point of it was. The anti-war message of the film seemed based on nothing more than the assertion that soldiers get horribly wounded in wars and that society doesn't pay sufficient regard to their plight. That is true, but not more true of the Vietnam War than of other wars. Furthermore, the film seemed to argue that liberals, even when they are disabled, make better and more sensitive lovers than conservatives. Sally signals her emotional and political development by having her first orgasm, which is an enticing if not necessarily plausible development of the anti-war argument.

Fonda's strategic allegiance had led her in a peculiar direction. In *Klute* she had – in her own performance at least – taken the processes of filmmaking and, most especially, acting apart. And she had famously said at the time that 'being a film star is not a purpose'. Moviemaking had no intrinsic importance, stardom was a sham, and was only of use insofar as it could be turned into a tool. Yet, in working with Godard, she had seen one possible result of rejecting movies, which was to lose your audience entirely. The arguments were what mattered. They had to be got across, and to the largest possible audience, which meant working in a popular form and making the argument itself palatable, even reassuring. Therefore,

Comes a Horseman (1978) was an elegaic Western in
which Jane Fonda uncannily resembled her father.

paradoxically, her despising of film forms had actually led her back to those very forms. In fact, her analysis discouraged her from developing the forms and making them more complex because all that mattered was reaching an audience. All her films since *Klute* had been wrong turnings: documentaries, radical new styles, highbrow classics, all these confined her to a ghetto. Even the complexities that she had captured so brilliantly in *Klute* were a distraction. There was no particular point in renewing an old form, however sensitively; after all, it was only cinema. She was now applying the standards of Hollywood at its most commercial, but with a different purpose. But then, even more paradoxically, in putting the emphasis in a film like *Coming Home* on the love story, the message got lost. So Jane Fonda was making the old style of commercial film but without the belief in them that gave them conviction.

Maybe that was why the film was such a success. The Vietnam War had been a taboo subject in Hollywood, largely because it was a cause of division. Who wanted a film aimed at half an audience? *Coming Home* managed to express the disquiet that both sides felt about the war, whether it was a basic (left-wing) distrust of the military, or a (right-wing) resentment at the treatment of returning veterans.

Fonda was working hard and successfully now. Almost in a mood of commemoration, she was reunited with the director of *Klute*, Alan J. Pakula, to make *Comes a Horseman*, a stark, austere Western in which she challenges comparison with her father. Then she appeared in one of the four episodes of *California Suite*, looking great in a bikini and swapping Neil Simon's brittle epigrams with Alan Alda.

Hollywood loves a comeback, it loves a film featuring disability, it loves pretending that it can deal with serious issues. *Coming Home*

On location for *California Suite* (1978) with director Herbert
Ross. She was apolitical, funny and looked great.

had it all and the major Oscars that year were divided between it and the other Vietnam film, *The Deer Hunter* (which Jane Fonda denounced without having seen). Jon Voight won the Oscar for best actor while she won her second Oscar for best actress. Hollywood also likes an eccentric acceptance speech, so long as it's short, and Fonda delivered her acknowledgements in sign language, saying (and signing) that they had all become more aware of the problems of the handicapped while making the film. She concluded her effusive speech by thanking her husband: 'He helped me to believe that besides being entertaining, movies can inspire and teach and even be healing.' Her rehabilitation was triumphantly complete, at least as far as Hollywood was concerned.

Chapter Five

COMING OF AGE

J ane Fonda, who has never been less than extraordinary, took immense pains to develop an image of ordinariness in the public view of her life with Tom Hayden. She portrayed herself in press interviews as a mother who looked after her house and sent her daughter to Sunday school: 'I fill with angst if the house isn't cleaned up'. She admitted that the tone of her radical anti-war protests had been 'inhuman and alienating'. From her very first interviews given when she was starring in *Tall Story*, she had been tirelessly analytical, and self-analytical. But now she was more conscious of what she wanted to achieve.

She insisted that film stars were overpaid: 'It's wrong that the rich keep getting richer. I'm earning close to one million dollars a movie and that's madness. But that is the system in Hollywood. Should I take less money? Should I stop acting? No. I deal with it in

Fonda in 1979: the first female Hollywood star to remain a romantic lead in her forties.

my own way. I try to live as simply as I can, and all my money goes into political work. I put it to better use than the big studios, so I take them for every penny they are foolish enough to give me.'

This money was largely used in the Campaign for Economic Democracy for a new kind of activism that was largely based in California, where they lived and where it would be most constructive for Hayden's career. But Fonda insisted on the continuity in her causes. In Vietnam she had (she now said) been combating American military imperialism: 'What I have been fighting in California is another kind of imperialism, the power of the US multinational corporations over one of our fundamental resources, namely food.'

Ever since the mid-seventies she had been a critic of the major food corporations, though the emphasis on non-unionised labour had gradually shifted to the nutritional content of the produce. The couple also targeted the nuclear industry, and this was a good example of the synergy that has always existed between Jane Fonda's various concerns, since the abuses of the nuclear industry also happened to be the subject of her new film.

After she had finished *Coming Home*, she proclaimed she had had her say on Vietnam, and that now there were 'other battlefields' she wanted to fight on. Two potential projects for IPC were especially close to her heart. The first was a film she planned to star in with her father and her brother, a family saga beginning in 1776 with the War of Independence and called *A House Divided*. But the bicentennial had passed and with it the moment for that film, and they never made it. The second idea she described was 'inspired by the true story of a woman who goes to work in a plutonium fast breeder reactor plant in Oklahoma and discovers that there's a cover-up to disguise the fact that fuel rods containing plutonium are faulty and could cause a cataclysmic kind of accident. The real woman did, in fact, die and we intend to point a finger at the person responsible for her death.'

Fonda was referring to the story of Karen Silkwood which was filmed by Mike Nichols in 1983 starring Meryl Streep. There are considerable problems in basing films on the lives of real people. They can, as Ron Kovic did, sell their story to somebody else or, as proved to be the case with the Silkwood story, it can be difficult to obtain the necessary legal clearances. Once more Fonda began with the true story of an individual and dropped it in favour of the story of the development of an apolitical innocent played by Jane Fonda, as if she were compelled to recapitulate her own career and coming of age over and over again. In *The China Syndrome*, Fonda played an ambitious but naïve TV reporter who while visiting a nuclear power station witnesses, and her cameraman (played by Michael Douglas) captures on film, a nuclear near-accident.

The story had been developed by a documentary filmmaker, Michael Gray, and sold to Michael Douglas who had cast Richard Dreyfuss in the lead. When Dreyfuss withdrew, Fonda stepped in, both as an actor and as co-producer. Just as she was now committed to traditional film forms, such as the thriller, the love story, the romantic comedy, so she also distrusted untried directors. She wanted reliable professionals and she had Gray replaced with the workmanlike James Bridges, who rewrote much of the script with her in mind. The producers maintained careful secrecy about the film's attitude to the industry so that they were, initially at least, able to shoot inside authentic nuclear plants. Considering Jane Fonda's highly public stance on the issue, their gullibility could be seen as further evidence of the nuclear industry's basic incompetence.

The China Syndrome is an effective thriller, with an especially powerful performance from Jack Lemmon as a senior engineer in the nuclear plant. Michael Gray had trained as a nuclear engineer and the film benefited greatly from this authority. Far from being a simplistic diatribe, one of the central issues in the film is the difficulty in public debate about the industry because of the scientific and engineering technicalities involved.

Ever since the Vietnam War had ended, and Richard Nixon had looked more likely than Jane Fonda to go to prison, it had seemed possible that American society might be moving her way. After *The China Syndrome* was released to not much effect, it seemed as if the studio's doubts about the incomprehensible title might prove justified (it referred to a theoretical possibility that in certain kinds of nuclear accident the core might melt down and become so hot that it would go through the earth all the way to China). But then it seemed as if fate, as well as history, was on Fonda's side. At the end of March 1979, two weeks after *The China Syndrome* opened, there was an accident at the Three Mile Island nuclear power station near Harrisburg, Pennsylvania. The safety features failed to work and contaminated steam was released into the atmosphere. It triggered a panic and a major news story.

There was a half-hearted attempt by the producers not to be seen to capitalise on the accident in too explicit a manner, especially as the publicity had already transformed the film into a major hit. Jack Lemmon refused outright to do any more publicity for the film. Fonda took a slightly different view. She welcomed links between the film and the accident and when, later that year, she and her husband began a speaking tour of the eastern half of the United States, they actually began it at Three Mile Island. Fonda has been

Jane Fonda with her co-stars in the nuclear thriller
The China Syndrome, Jack Lemmon and Michael Douglas.

criticised for this but weren't her actions more consistent than those of Jack Lemmon? By his own account, Lemmon had not only taken the role but also turned down work for a year before shooting started to make sure he was available for it because he shared the distrust of the nuclear industry dramatised by Michael Gray. Then, when those fears were realised, he pulled back. Was this sensitivity or was it the old Hollywood fear of taking a position on any issue that might provoke controversy? Fonda saw that the conjunction of the film and the accident provided the opportunity for a devastating campaign against the industry, and she rightly seized it while her colleagues headed for cover.

Fonda and Hayden had formed a close relationship with Jerry Brown, the liberal, not to say bohemian, governor of California. In return for the substantial money they raised for his gubernatorial campaign, he appointed several members of their CED to his office, including Hayden himself, who became Brown's energy adviser (to the dismay of the state's energy companies). In March 1979 he appointed Fonda to the California Arts Council. The appointment of the most successful actress in Hollywood to such a post might be considered uncontroversial enough, and it might be thought that the furore over *The China Syndrome* would only reinforce Fonda's claims. But few events in Fonda's life have passed quietly or without controversy.

As a response to increasing reports of atrocities in what was now the Socialist Republic of Vietnam, Joan Baez, the singer, activist and ex-associate of Fonda had formed a human rights organisation called Humanitas. It conducted research into reports of human rights violations and found strong evidence to confirm them. (These were reinforced when Vietnamese citizens began to take to

Tom Hayden's political career always depended on his
famous wife's wealth and influence...

...but did her charisma expose his shortcomings? Hayden
addresses a 1979 anti-nuclear rally while Fonda applauds.

the seas in flimsy boats in desperate attempts to escape their own country.) An open letter headed 'An Appeal to the Conscience of Vietnam' condemning these abuses was published in newspapers and signed by Baez and other well-known figures on the left, such as Ed Asner, Lily Tomlin, Norman Lear (creator of *All in the Family*) and the union organizer Cesar Chavez.

Other well-known radicals, Daniel Ellsberg and Tom Hayden among them, refused to sign the petition, but Jane Fonda went further, writing a barely coherent open letter of her own in rebuttal of Baez. She questioned the reliability of Baez's sources and her definition of repression. She denied that any bloodbath had occurred:

> *I hope you will reconsider the assertion of your ad: That the Vietnamese people are waiting to die. Such rhetoric only aligns you with the most narrow and negative element in our country who continue to believe that communism is worse than death. This 'better dead than Red' philosophy originated with Cardinal Spellman and John Foster Dulles and it shocks me that you have come full circle to their original assumption. The assumption that led to the war and the slaughter.*

It was not necessary to be a supporter of America's conduct of the Vietnam War to be dismayed by Fonda's refusal to accept evidence of atrocities that seemed irrefutable. In response, Baez was able to take on the role of the sorrowful ex-friend and admirer: 'After all, she risked her career for what she believed. But, I was never really comfortable with some of the things she did, being pictured holding an M-16, or whatever that thing was.'

The controversy over Fonda's job only increased when she secured a prestigious post for Edison Miller, an associate of hers, in California's conservative Orange County. Miller was a colonel who, as a prisoner of war, had willingly appeared alongside her and denounced the American presence in Vietnam. He had been dismissed from the US Marines and assaulted by fellow prisoners. A Republican Senator, Bob Nimmo, commented in response: 'In my view she is a traitor to this country. And this Miller business – Brown's running for president, do we want a president who's advised by traitors and collaborators?' Nancy Reagan, who a year later would be the president's wife, described the appointment as 'an insult to every former POW'.

The California Senate promptly voted by twenty-eight to five to reject her own appointment to the Arts Council. An open letter in support of Fonda was signed by the most famous actors in Hollywood and published in newspapers, but the Californian public overwhelmingly supported the veto.

This rejection was a defining moment in Jane Fonda's career. A year earlier she had given a triumphant interview about her comeback in which she had expressed her determination to show that she could flourish in spite of all the controversy that continued to dog her: 'There's a stereotype in people's minds that if you're politically active for social change then you're going to suffer as an artist because somehow you can't do both. I want to keep going to avoid any chance of a subliminal message getting out that "they did her in". People root for a survivor who sticks her neck out. Maybe I represent someone who fights back and doesn't stop and still survives.'

She had now discovered that, though her rehabilitation was remarkable, it was still severely circumscribed. The Hollywood community was far more willing to forgive than the public at large. There was a difference between accepting her as a movie star and agreeing with her, liking her or forgiving her. It was tempting to take the box-office success of *Coming Home* and *The China Syndrome* as a sign that the American people were coming to share her political views, but this was misleading in every way. The American public was united in being opposed to the callous neglect of disabled war veterans and equally united in its disapproval of nuclear accidents being concealed by faked photographs, but Jane Fonda's audience was also about to elect Ronald Reagan to two terms as President.

She must have realised that the Hanoi journey was her Watergate, her Chappaquiddick. It would always be raised against her and there was no restitution that would satisfy her opponents, even if she were willing to make it. She remained a huge movie star, a 1980 Gallup poll named her as one of the world's ten most admired women, but if she couldn't survive a month on the California Arts Council, then it was clear that she would have to exercise her influence outside the orthodox political system.

But what about Tom Hayden? He had been in Hanoi too, but in this case his lack of allure had served him well. An associate once described him as having 'the charisma of an iguana', and there was something of a facial resemblance as well. The Vietcong photographer had not apparently been as keen to pose Hayden next to the guns, or maybe he had prudently edged himself out of the frame. The question for Fonda now was whether she was most effectively advancing her cause through Tom Hayden's sluggish political progress or her own still dazzling movie career. The two were far from independent of each other. The CED, on which his political organization depended, required a large amount of money from

Jane Fonda and Robert Redford, pleasantly reunited in
The Electric Horseman (1979).

Fonda's earnings, and he once made a not very funny joke about her having to maximise them before she was too old.

There was no immediate sign of that. She looked better than ever in *The Electric Horseman*, in which she starred opposite Robert Redford. This was a production by Redford for which she was hired (at a third of his salary), but since he shared many of her views, it followed a similar progress. Redford plays an ageing rodeo rider who has been hired, along with his horse, by a corporation to advertise breakfast cereal and promote a new casino in Las Vegas. When he discovers that the horse has been drugged to keep it docile, he rides it away and out on to the prairie. Fonda plays a TV journalist who pursues him for the story and is won over by him. It's a flimsy but enjoyable film, and it suggested that Fonda could now act with a lighter touch when she was working for somebody else. It was difficult not to feel dissatisfied by it as well. Fonda had worked with Redford twelve years earlier in *Barefoot in the Park* and with the director, Sydney Pollack, ten years earlier in *They Shoot Horses, Don't They?* If anything, Fonda was now better looking than she had been in her twenties, as if she now looked the way she wanted to look and was content with her age, but her acting lacked the brio of the Fonda of the mid-sixties. And, amiable though she was, it was like a glimpse of what her career might have been if she had never made *Klute*. With any other female movie star, this would have been a necessity because of a lack of control. But these were the parts Fonda had chosen to play. She was now being a role model for middle-aged women, and that was something, but it was at the expense of being an actress.

Perhaps this argument is beside the point. When she formed her production company with Bruce Gilbert, she was explicit about

In the wake of *Nine to Five*'s release, Fonda appears at
a rally to mark National Secretaries' Day.

Lily Tomlin, Jane Fonda and Dolly Parton in costume for *Nine to Five* (1980), the most financially successful Fonda production.

The same actresses looking triumphant at the premiere of *Nine to Five*.

their way of working: 'We begin with a particular subject we want to tackle and then formulate a story around it. Then we go out and hire a writer.' This was certainly true of her next project, which began as research about the exploitation of women in the workplace. Fonda herself interviewed female office-workers and then hired a writer, Patricia Resnick, who went and worked in an office herself to gather material. Yet the result of the genuinely startling findings about prejudicial and exploitative treatment was not the tough exposé one might have expected. In Fonda's own words it was 'a "labor film", but I hope of a new kind, different from *The Grapes of Wrath* or *Salt of the Earth.*' This was undeniable. Fonda was now 'supersensitive to anything that smacks of the soapbox or lecturing the audience' and all that research and anger at sexual oppression resulted in the empty-headed, frothy comedy, *Nine to Five*, in which Fonda starred with Dolly Parton and Lily Tomlin as three beleaguered secretaries who take revenge on their boss. It was a crude, ugly-looking comedy, and as Pauline Kael said of Fonda, 'it's not much fun watching her get politicized all over again. (Three productions, three losses of innocence.)' And four, if you counted *The Electric Horseman.*

Nine to Five was the biggest hit of Fonda's career so far, earning over a hundred million dollars at the box office and spawning in its turn a television situation comedy. This was unsurprising because the film itself resembled a TV comedy, and perhaps that was a mark of Fonda's achievement in packaging her ideas. Perhaps it was further evidence of her devotion to these ideas that she was overshadowed by her two co-stars to an extent unparallelled in her career.

Her next film role was entirely different. She did not initiate it, it was not political, she was not the star, and it was a script passed on to her by her father. Finally, and it would without any doubt be finally because Henry Fonda was now aged and ill, she would have the chance to make a film with her father.

Ernest Thompson's play, *On Golden Pond*, was produced off-Broadway in the autumn of 1978. It is about a summer that an old couple spend, as always, in their holiday house by a lake. The man is going deaf, losing his memory and is bad tempered, but we are meant to see his fundamental goodness and the deep love he and his wife feel for each other. His daughter and her new lover drop his son off with the couple while they spend a month in Europe, and in that month the old man forges a relationship with the boy and the characters achieve a new understanding of each other and themselves.

The attraction of the play for grand old actors was obvious, and Katharine Hepburn had already expressed her wish to play the wife. One of the play's producers sent the script to Henry Fonda who was also keen. He passed it on to his daughter, and she agreed to produce the film and play the part of Chelsea, the old man's partly estranged daughter, who reaches a new intimacy at the end with her father. For Jane, the idea was irresistible: it would allow her to work with her father on her own terms, yet giving him the most substantial role he had had for years; it might allow them to reach a new closeness, or at least they would have to act as if it did. A relationship that had been confused from the beginning between the idealised image on a screen and the flawed reality would conclude by fusing the two into one. The reconciliation that Chelsea and Norman achieve would simultaneously be the ultimate reconciliation between Jane and Henry.

The shooting of the film was a battle of styles, reflecting a deeply held difference in convictions about acting technique that went back to Jane's days at the Actors Studio and that in its turn reflected a contrast in personality. Henry Fonda believed in stoicism, privacy in his own life and professional detachment in his performance. Jane Fonda believed in openness, and a life where politics, her profession and her private life were inextricable. In the shooting of the film, she wanted an emotional, improvisatory closeness while he remained detached. So did Katharine Hepburn. It was as if Jane Fonda still believed in a Hollywood myth that they had grown out of. Hepburn briskly refused to be sentimental about working with Henry Fonda for the first time: 'Henry Fonda's not one to make new friends, and neither am I, but we got along okay. He has his own world. He likes to sit and fish, I like to walk through the woods alone. We are quite similar. He doesn't waste time. No small talk. And I hate to have idiotic conversations. We found we could act together just like *that!*'

But even Hepburn stayed after her own scenes were finished in order to be present for the shooting of the reconciliation scene between the father and daughter, and she acknowledged that there was an extra layer of meaning behind it for everybody, for Henry and Jane, but also for the rest of us because stars like Henry and Jane Fonda belong to all of us: 'They're both reaching for something they think they've missed.'

In terms of their personal relationship, that final scene was everything Jane wanted it to be, as even her father admitted. When the shot was completed everybody on the set, more than thirty of them, was in tears. 'I'm not a religious man,' Fonda said later. 'But I thank God every morning that I lived long enough to play that role.'

There was scarcely a need to count the votes at the Academy Awards ceremony after the film was released. The film was about an old man near death and Henry Fonda was dying, this was his last film, he had never won an Oscar before, it was about Henry and Jane hugging each other. Of course he won the Oscar (the Academy threw in an Oscar for Katharine Hepburn as well) and, since he was too ill to receive it in person, of course Jane picked it up for him. And there was always a vein of shrewdness in Jane Fonda even when she was at her most emotional. *On Golden Pond* was the top-grossing film of 1981 and the most profitable film IPC ever made.

On Golden Pond was part of the luck that Henry Fonda had had for most of his career, and for once an example of luck in his personal life as well. He died on 11 August 1982, fulfilled, rewarded and publicly adored by his famous and successful daughter. For Jane Fonda as well, there was a sense in which the film closed a circle that had begun in the spring of 1955 when Jane had acted with her father in a charity production of Clifford Odets' play, *The Country Girl*. But the question of whether the film was as good for Jane Fonda as it was for her father is more difficult to answer.

As so often, the honours showered on *On Golden Pond* said more about what people wanted to find in the film than the film itself. How could this not be so? Henry Fonda and Katharine Hepburn are a part of all our lives, and the symbolism of having them together and the clash of generations with Jane Fonda as their daughter was irresistible and made it difficult to point out that the film itself is crudely manipulative, trading on unearned emotion, and poorly acted even by the two stars. Audiences and critics were so eager to applaud the aged Henry Fonda that they paid little heed to his curiously unpleasant performance that goes beyond the crotchetiness we are meant to find adorable.

It is heartwarming to learn from the various participants that Henry and Jane Fonda achieved a new emotional contact during the shooting of the film but, unlike in *Klute*, this emotional reality gave no actual (as opposed to symbolic) benefit to what we see on screen. It seems to have had the opposite effect. Jane Fonda's performance as Chelsea is by some way the poorest of her career. She has said that she was intimidated by the prospect of working with these two great veterans, but she had talked of being nervous before, especially in her earlier films. But what is striking about her early performances is their assurance. In *On Golden Pond* she really does look ill-at-ease. With Norman's horrible taunting of her, she was evidently having to re-enact some of her most terrible childhood experiences and she couldn't do it, or at least couldn't do it well. Perhaps it was too painful, perhaps she was no longer willing to expose herself as an actress in the way she once had, or maybe it was just a practical matter. Her father and Hepburn were frail and couldn't do many takes, let alone make use of the improvisatory style that might have loosened up her performance.

On Golden Pond was the end of Henry Fonda's career as a movie star, and in a way it was the end of Jane Fonda's as well. Though she made five more films, not only were they flops but her performances were tentative and unsatisfactory. It is tempting to look for psychological explanations, as if Jane could only flourish as an actress while Henry was alive, because it freed her to be the delinquent daughter rebelling against authority. Once her father was gone, this no longer seemed possible.

For other actresses, the tailing off of a great career would have been a disaster, but Jane Fonda has never been other actresses. By the time this was happening, she already had a new career that was even bigger.

Chapter Six

WORKING OUT

However much she talked about women learning to love their wrinkles, Fonda knew that she might well be approaching the end of her life as a major movie star. What should she do next? At various times she considered starting a restaurant chain or a network of car-repairers that wouldn't rip women off. But she was warned against committing resources to any area that she didn't really understand. The most sensible course would be to develop something she was already doing into a business.

In 1978 she had broken her foot and was unable to do the ballet exercises she had previously used to keep fit. She still needed to get in shape for the bikini scenes in *California Suite*, so she began working out in an exercise studio in Los Angeles that was part of a national chain owned by a fitness instructor called Gilda Marx. The

Jane Fonda in 1980, repositioning herself. It was a look that would define the decade.

idea occurred to her that, though opinions may have differed about her recent films, everybody agreed that she looked in terrific shape (especially in *California Suite*). Irony of ironies, Jane Fonda had spent a decade as the most famous activist in Hollywood, and at the end of it, her female admirers were more interested in emulating her physique than her political ideas. Still, it was an opportunity. Jane Fonda had always complained about the Hollywood obsession with idiotic, pretty, unthreatening female youthfulness. Now it seemed that she had become an admired symbol of female maturity.

Once more, Fonda showed her knack for bringing her convictions and her professional life together. In 1979 she opened the first Jane Fonda Workout Studio near Rodeo Drive in Los Angeles. It was cheap – $6 an hour at the beginning – and it was clearly defined in its aims. This was not a health club. Women went there to do basic, intense workout routines without complicated apparatus. They didn't go there to swim or to eat lunch. She said she wanted to invest 'in something watertight' and she insisted on its lack of controversy: 'It is not political, it doesn't harm anyone. Quite the contrary, it's beneficial for most people: it makes them feel good.' It may not have been an obviously ideological venture but, as always, Fonda made it seem more like a crusade than a business plan: 'I'm not trying to look young,' she told the press. 'I disapprove of the youth cult. I like women looking their age.' And when working women rushed into the Workout Studio for some lunchtime aerobics, they passed a sign in the lobby that read: 'Profits from The Workout support the Campaign for Economic Democracy in its efforts to promote alternative sources of energy, stop environmental cancer and fight for women's rights, justice for tenants and other causes related to environmental protection, social justice and world peace.'

Fonda was quickly proved right about the watertightness of her investment. It was an immediate success and the initial $200,000 was earned back after a mere six months. With perfect timing, Jane Fonda had launched her new career on the eve of what Tom Wolfe would christen the 'Me Decade', a culture in which politics seemed to give way to personal development, consumerism, health and exercise. This has sometimes been portrayed as a contrast to the supposed idealism of the sixties, but it might more plausibly be seen as its logical development. The members of the baby boom generation who had been dodging the draft, taking drugs, having sex and listening to pop music as teenagers, were now middle aged and more interested in keeping in shape and eating right. And where they had previously needed to borrow money, resentfully, from their parents, now they had disposable income of their own. If they were unwilling to donate money directly to the Campaign for Economic Democracy, then they could do so indirectly, and probably unknowingly.

Fonda quickly opened a second and then a third Workout Studio, but if she had thought she was invulnerable, then her next film showed otherwise. On the face of it, it had all the characteristics of another success. Fonda always had a gift for spotting trends early and *Rollover* was a prescient Wall Street thriller at the beginning of a decade when the financial sector would assume a higher profile in the economy than ever before. It was directed by Alan J. Pakula, who had worked with Fonda twice previously and who had shown a capacity to maintain narrative drive in labyrinthine conspiracy thrillers twice before (in *The Parallax View* and *All the President's Men*). This time his touch deserted him, and he produced a clotted tale that managed to make the collapse of the entire world economy seem uninvolving. Pakula is celebrated for his skill with actors, which

Fonda with Kris Kristofferson in *Rollover* (1981), a box-office
flop that devastated her.

made the failings of the two stars even less explicable. Admittedly, Kris Kristofferson had made his name portraying outlaws and other low-lifes and was never going to be convincing as a Wall Street supertrader, but Fonda too seemed unhappy as an ex-actress and high-society dame rather than in her traditional role of an innocent junior reporter. Whatever the reason, the film was IPC's first outright flop. It was released in the same year as *On Golden Pond*, and this quiet film which she had made as a gesture towards her father took about twenty times as much at the box office as her overtly commercial thriller. This failure, after such a run of success, hurt Fonda deeply. She didn't make another film for four years and it marked the end of her association with Bruce Gilbert and of IPC films itself. The IPC formula had been based on tailoring everything to box-office success. If that failed, what was left?

Fonda's Midas touch was apparently now reserved for the fitness industry. The success of the Workout studios continued and in 1982 she published *Jane Fonda's Workout Book*, which was also a triumph, selling almost two million hardback copies within a year. A second fitness book, *Jane Fonda's Workout Book for Pregnancy, Birth and Recovery*, became another bestseller.

She was then approached by a young video producer, Stuart Karl, who suggested she do a video for sale. There were lots of good reasons for not doing this. Most videos were rented, not sold, it was risky to give away all the secrets of the fitness programme for the price of just a couple of visits to a Workout Studio. And if film stars were supposed to resist appearing on television, wasn't it even more of a comedown to make a video, with all its associations of cheapness? Fonda did it anyway, and records and tapes as well, and they all sold hugely. Her performance in these videos was a remarkable combination of the bright-eyed, sprightly ingenue of her early Hollywood days and the earnest political agitator, inciting her audiences to better themselves. As if in Richard Nixon's worst nightmare, Jane Fonda got into almost every home in America and told its women what to do, and they obeyed, at least for a few days until they gave up and the Workout video slipped to the bottom of the pile. For a few years in the early eighties, Fonda seemed omnipresent and the leotard joined the pin-striped suit as the emblematic costume of the decade.

What had begun as an investment had turned into an industry that by the end of 1982 had earned more than $20 million. In a complicated arrangement, Workout Inc. was owned by the Campaign for Economic Democracy though legal rights were retained by Fonda. Certainly there was no doubt that the CED depended almost entirely on the Workout business: in 1982, for example, it received $300,000. The CED, in turn, contributed to Tom Hayden's campaign in that year to be Democratic representative in the 44th District of the California State Assembly, the district which included Santa Monica, West Los Angeles and Malibu and contained some of the poorest and richest housing areas in the country. Hayden's campaign was nominally separate from the CED, though he said his policies overlapped with the organisation's on issues 'such as solar energy, investment of pension funds in housing and high-technology industries, support for working women's organisations, social services for senior citizens, offshore oil drilling and smog'.

Despite the huge support from his wife, Hayden's progress even to this relatively humble elective office was far from straight-forward. His Jewish opponent for the pre-election nomination damagingly accused him of being soft on the PLO, so – as if in some surreal mirror-image of their trip to Hanoi – Hayden and Fonda travelled to Israel to proclaim their support for the Israeli invasion of the Lebanon. The two of them actually went close to the front lines in Lebanon and approvingly watched the big guns of the Israeli army shelling West Beirut. Back in the United States he announced that he was an 'ex-socialist' and in favour of the death penalty: 'I'm not the angry young man I used to be,' he said in his campaign TV commercial. Hayden narrowly won the nomination and then the election itself, achieving public office for the first time at the age of forty-one. His election had cost $1.3 million, almost half of which had been contributed by his wife (and this doesn't include the funds he had received from the CED), and all for a local political post which paid a salary of $42,000.

What is more, Hayden only just avoided suffering the ignominy of being ejected from the Assembly within days of taking his seat. A Republican Representative tabled a bizarre motion claiming that the state constitution forbade traitors from becoming representatives; this, probably illegal, challenge was only defeated by forty-one votes to thirty-six.

Altogether, it was something of a pyrrhic victory. At the beginning of the campaign, there had been wild, if barely expressed, hopes that this might be the beginning of a trail that would end with Hayden and Fonda in the White House. Now it was clear that Hayden would require prudence and money just to cling on to the little he had achieved. Hayden's political future lay not as a prominent national figure but as a political networker, a figure of influence behind the scenes, on committees, advising, writing speeches. That was not to be despised, and a local politician in California, with its immense size and wealth, could achieve a great deal, but it wasn't what Fonda and Hayden had had in mind when they met. From now on, Hayden would devote more of his time to the nitty-gritty, organisational side of politics, at which he excelled and to which Fonda had less to contribute. This also meant spending most of his time in Sacramento where the Californian State Assembly was based.

Fonda, for her own part, devoted herself to the inevitable stresses of what was now a major business. In 1983 the *Daily Mail* claimed that Fonda had suffered a heart attack. This false rumour showed how much the company depended on Fonda's highly toned, supple body, and in order to refute it she performed a tough work-out in front of reporters. There were other pressures. Gilda Marx, at whose studio Fonda had first worked out, claimed that the ideas and techniques of Workout had been stolen from her. A leisure-clothing operation started and then failed. But the core operation still prospered. The original Workout book was on the bestseller lists for more than three years and then, when *Jane Fonda's Low Impact Aerobic Workout* was a bestseller as well, Joan Rivers observed that Fonda 'didn't get that terrific body from exercising. She got it from lifting all that money.'

By 1985 Fonda had established herself as one of the most successful and influential women in the world. The rest of the decade would be more of a trial. She was approaching fifty, and if she was going to keep embodying, indeed to some extent inventing, attractive images of ageing women, she would have to find the film roles to go with them. For *Agnes of God* in 1985 she played a psychiatrist who goes to a convent where a young nun has had a baby and killed it. The movie had a certain theatrical power (it was based on a stage play by John Pielmeier), but the drama of the conflict between her rationality and the cloistered religious world was routine. This minor

Fonda seemed ill at ease playing the role of a
socialite ex-actress in *Rollover*.

Fonda and Anne Bancroft enjoying a light moment on the set of
Agnes of God, a film about a nun who has killed her baby.

work wasn't going to do anything for its star, though she said that working on it had brought her a new religious faith.

Her next film was a promisingly unpretentious thriller, *The Morning After*, directed by Sidney Lumet (who had directed Henry Fonda in *Twelve Angry Men*). Fonda plays Alex, an actress whose career has been ruined by drinking. The film begins as she wakes up, hung over and unable to remember how she got there, and discovers that the man beside her has been murdered. She gives a rough, funny performance and works well with her costar, Jeff Bridges. The pity is that she was working with Lumet in a period of his career (which is still not over) when he was making a succession of misfired movies. *The Morning After* had been rewritten to death, and after a promising start it slides into inanity. The failures were mounting up and they were more damaging than they would have been to a Jane Fonda in her twenties or thirties.

Jane Fonda's film career was terminated by the experience of the two films she made one after another at the end of the decade. She was a friend of the distinguished Mexican novelist Carlos Fuentes, and in 1981 he showed her his work-in-progress, *The Old Gringo*, which takes off from the true story of the American writer Ambrose Bierce, who as an old man in 1913 travelled to Mexico and disappeared, probably killed in the civil war. Fonda was intrigued by the idea of a drama about the strange, rich, violent relationship between the United States and Mexico, and told Fuentes that she hoped there would be a character in the story she could play. The completed novel was about a middle-aged female American school-teacher in Mexico who becomes involved both with the old gringo (American) of the title and a handsome young Mexican rebel soldier. Fonda immediately optioned the book. But it presented exceptional

Fonda in Sidney Lumet's thriller *The Morning After* (1986), for
which she got an Oscar nomination.

challenges to any screen adaptation. It was an elusive, difficult work that took place largely in the minds of the characters. She commissioned a screenplay and then numerous rewrites from the husband-and-wife team, Joan Didion and John Gregory Dunne. Then, when she changed directors, the new director, Luis Puenzo, wrote a new screenplay from scratch.

There were problems during shooting. Burt Lancaster, the original choice to play Bierce, was refused insurance and had to be replaced by Gregory Peck. But the Mexican rebel was played by Jimmy Smits, the new TV star from *LA Law*, and it seemed as if this might be the big success that would re-establish Fonda as a movie star once again. It was a film of great importance to her, it had taken eight years to bring to the screen, it was the first film produced by the new company, Fonda Films, and she promoted the film with immense energy, discussing it as if she was on the couch: 'I am vulnerable and I bring that to every part I play. I like characters that are complex. I wouldn't play a woman who was just weak, and I certainly wouldn't want to act a woman who was totally resolved and lacking in contradictions.'

Maybe the book itself was intractable – John Updike described it harshly as 'a very stilted effort, static and wordy, a series of tableaux costumed in fustian and tinted a kind of sepia' – but *Old Gringo* (as the film was very slightly retitled) just isn't very good, and Fonda's own performance is a little sad. She was in her fifties now, and it seems a bit undignified for her to be trying to play a thirty-five-year-old spinster (in the original book she is thirty). The film had been so long in the loving nurturing that the reason for making it had been lost somewhere along the way. It's a story about revolution and about a woman who leaves Boston respectability and

Jane Fonda with director Sidney Lumet on the set of
The Morning After. She gave a fine performance but
the film itself disappointed.

With co-star Jimmy Smits in *Old Gringo* (1989). Its failure
coincided with the break-up of her marriage to Tom Hayden.

goes into the dirty and sensual world of Mexico, yet Fonda is ethereal and glowing where she should be aroused and scared.

She went straight from *Old Gringo* to an even more difficult experience, starring opposite Robert De Niro in *Stanley and Iris*. There were no problems with the film itself, which was merely an (unintentionally) amusing example of an absurd Hollywood adaptation. Pat Barker's original novel, *Union Street*, about seven working-class women in a northern English town during the 1973 miners' strike became a tiresomely sentimental story set in a Connecticut town about a female factory worker teaching an illiterate colleague to read.

When it was announced that the film would be shot on location in Waterbury, Connecticut, there were some isolated protests by war veterans about the presence of Fonda. She was used to this, but this time they attracted support and began a controversy about whether Fonda should be allowed to work in the town at all, or even whether she should still be indicted for treason. It became a national news story and there were discussions on television, all of which made use of film footage of Fonda with the anti-aircraft gun. Fonda sprang into action. She gave a faltering, uncomfortable interview on national television with Barbara Walters in which she expressed certain regrets, if not apologies. Tom Hayden flew in and addressed some local people. Finally, Fonda herself went to a crowded meeting of her most bitter critics and spent three hours with them defending herself. She promised to attend a charity event for sufferers from the chemical, Agent Orange, which had been dropped on Vietnam (in order to strip it of vegetation). A small group of her enemies was not won over and continued to demonstrate throughout the shooting of the film, but it could now go ahead.

The generation which had protested against Vietnam was now in middle age and taking its place in the political establishment. Fonda had once talked of Tom Hayden being president in 1992 and in fact the winner of the 1992 election would be a man who had deliberately avoided the draft (following a Republican vice-president, Dan Quayle, who had avoided going to Vietnam by joining the National Guard). Other people's radical youth could be explained away or justified or apologised for or just forgotten about, but Jane Fonda seemed to be the exception. The carefully nurtured image of moderation, the insistence on ordinariness, the devotion to issues of lifestyle, and the passing of sixteen years, all counted for nothing. It may have been, as she told Barbara Walters, that because of her visibility she had become the lightning rod for people's anguish over the war. Her opponents, and even some who were also in the anti-war movement, would say that she decisively crossed a boundary from legitimate campaigning for a withdrawal of US forces to a support for her country's enemies and hoping that US troops be defeated in battle. In this context, it should be remembered that even in the mid-nineties, the proposal to rename a street in Berlin after Marlene Dietrich met with opposition because some local people believed that by supporting allied forces against the armies of the Third Reich she was being a traitor to her country. Female movie stars are visible, and Jane Fonda has always been highly visible even among female movie stars. She brought much the same flair and enthusiasm to mounting a gun near Hanoi that she brought to stretching in a leotard, and both images proved unforgettable. As a young woman (though not *that* young – she was thirty-four), she had set out to become one of the most famous radicals in the world, and she succeeded, as she had succeeded at almost everything she put her

With Robert De Niro in *Stanley and Iris*. Shooting was marred by protests against her Hanoi visit almost 20 years earlier.

mind to. For years she had struggled to make herself uncontroversial, and she had failed. That was something she would never be. It was a blow to her and it was a blow to her marriage, which had been based on their mutual sense of purpose.

In the second half of the eighties there had been an increased defensiveness about Jane Fonda's public pronouncements. It was in the nature of the peculiar, highly personal industry she had created that it depended on her own body. She had shown how middle-aged women could look good by staying fit and healthy. What even Jane Fonda couldn't do was stop women growing old and it seemed to make her angry:

> *I'm really appalled by what I see going on in plastic surgery in this country. We've got to make friends with those wrinkles and sags and grey hairs. We've got to understand they represent our lifetime experience. We see these women who have been nipped and tucked and injected and peeled to within an inch of their shiny, taut lives. Are they beautiful? No! Where is the personality, the life experience? It's gone. Besides, you can spot an inflated breast a mile away.*

Maybe she was protesting too much. She had always held up her private experiences as examples in her public life and this seemed more of a problem now that she and Hayden were spending more time apart and there were rumours of infidelity on both sides. The gap of three years between Fonda (born 1937) and Hayden (born 1940) may have seemed larger as she approached fifty. In January 1987 she gave an interview admitting her vulnerability: 'I feel some angst, let's face it, it's a youth-oriented culture and we're used to hearing doors clanging shut. So yes, I feel vulnerable.'

Jane Fonda in *Stanley and Iris* (1989), the final
film of her career.

By the middle of the year her appearance had changed start-
lingly. In conditions of secrecy, she had fat surgically removed
from around her upper and lower eyelids and then she had breast
implants done. After the operation, carried out in February 1987,
she was unable to work out for three weeks. There was also a
persistent rumour that she had had two of her ribs removed to
improve her figure, but this she has always strenuously denied. It
said a lot for the symbolic importance of Jane Fonda for millions
of women that her decision to have cosmetic surgery was a news
story around the world, and years later she was having to defend
it, the way she had to defend her Hanoi visit: 'I never said I would
never have plastic surgery. I said you have to make friends with the
ageing process and with your wrinkles, and you have to do everything you can. Especially for women who are in job markets where
youth is important. If you're going to have plastic surgery, this is
a serious decision. And you'd better do it properly, get references,
make sure they belong to such and such an organization. You
don't just look in the Yellow Pages.' You can almost sense a new
video coming.

Yet once again, Fonda, the most pragmatic of revolutionaries,
had squarely faced a contradiction that other people pretended
didn't exist. How do you get your message across in movies? By
trying to make a different sort of film or by making an old kind of
film with a new message? How do women deal with a world in which
youth and glamour are valued above qualities of intelligence and
maturity? By defying it in an almost certainly doomed attempt to
change society's attitudes or by going along with it? Or, like most
people and even Fonda herself in the end, by a bit of both and
muddling along out of all sorts of motives of insecurity.

Jane Fonda looking beautiful, but looking her age.

If Fonda had remodelled her body as a way of guaranteeing success with her new movies and saving her marriage, then it failed in every way. Both *Old Gringo* and *Stanley and Iris* were critically panned and performed poorly at the box office. The failure of *Old Gringo* was particularly painful, since it was the first film of her career that she had been entirely responsible for from beginning to end. This coincided with personal pressures. Rumours that she was having an affair with her co-star, Jimmy Smits, brought Hayden to the film set in Mexico. But it was Hayden's infidelity that brought the marriage to an end. There had been reports of affairs before, and Fonda hired a private detective to check on them. Hayden was working on the disastrous Michael Dukakis presidential campaign and he began a public liaison with Vickie Rideout, a thirty-one-year-old speech writer, and this Fonda couldn't ignore. They separated and immediately began to negotiate a divorce settlement. Fonda faced the possibility of having to divide her wealth with Hayden.

Hayden filed for divorce on 1 December 1989. She counter-sued two weeks later. The arguments between Fonda and Hayden and their lawyers were extremely acrimonious. Although Fonda had contributed millions of dollars to Hayden's political campaigns throughout their marriage, his lawyers insisted that this counted as a gift and had no relevance to the divorce settlement. Fonda may have been sourly amused that the technicality allowing her to give so much money to Hayden also entitled him to millions more of her money. Both sides had the capacity to harm the other by revealing private behaviour that might conflict with the public image. She offered a settlement of five million dollars. The estimates of what Hayden ended up with range from three million dollars plus an allowance of $200,000 a year to an outright payment of ten million dollars. Among the few comforts left by the angry end of their marriage may have been the thought that Hayden was now scarcely more likely than Roger Vadim to become US President.

Jane Fonda was devastated in a way that she had never been before, not even by the suicide of her mother, and, uncoincidentally, there were also problems with both her children. In the year of her separation from Hayden, her daughter Vanessa was arrested with her boyfriend and charged with attempting to buy drugs. Then in January 1990, the now sixteen-year-old Troy Hayden was arrested for spray-painting phone booths and walls in Los Angeles.

Fonda's film career seemed (and has proved to be) over. Her fitness career would at least be limited as she grew old. Her marriage had broken down. This seemed, finally, to be a crisis that would be too much even for Fonda. She embarked on a couple of casual affairs (one was with a young Italian bodybuilder) and gave some frankly confessional interviews, as if the process of development and growth could only occur in public. She wondered if she and Hayden had been too dependent on each other. Perhaps you needed self-sufficiency to make a marriage survive: 'And when you come together it is as two solitary wholenesses which can unite in a much firmer, more positive way. When you are a more integrated human being, then perhaps you can find another person.'

Was it a sign of hope or of maturity that this woman in her mid-fifties was still talking about learning how to live as she had been thirty years earlier? 'That hasn't happened to me yet, but I have every confidence that it will now. Will there be a good ending to the Jane Fonda story? Absolutely.' Then the phone rang.

Chapter Seven

JANE
& TED

ed Turner seems to have decided that Jane Fonda was the woman for him from the moment he heard of the break-up of her second marriage. As founder of CNN, Turner was one of the richest and most famous media figures in the world and about to become even more so with the triumph of the News Network in its reports on the Gulf War. He had once been known as a maverick businessman and yachtsman, most famous for winning the America's Cup in 1977. Now he was a global presence, who was used to dealing with national figures on equal terms. Jane Fonda was one of the few women in the world who was a match for him in wealth, power and glamour. And suddenly she was available.

He may also have sensed that they had much in common. They were both the products of middle-class families who had shunned quiet respectability. They both, gloriously, had something of the

The power couple: Jane Fonda and Ted Turner share a private moment at the entrance to the 1995 Oscars.

Ted Turner and his consort arrive to meet Queen Elizabeth II
and her consort in Washington D.C. in 1991.

huckster about them, a phenomenal drive that had taken them to triumph in more than one field. Both had experienced the suicide of a parent, and there was a consequent sense that the passion and inspiration on which they had built their lives had its dark, flawed side. Both had two failed marriages behind them, largely, it seemed because of the difficulty of finding a partner who could survive the proximity of such energy. Roger Vadim's film career never recovered from all the help he had been given by his wife. Likewise, it seemed that each vast financial contribution made by Fonda to her second husband's campaigns, each glittering personal appearance, only served to expose Hayden's own dourness. Vadim apparently didn't mind being overshadowed, Hayden finally felt humiliated, in each case the marriage ended.

Perhaps, once again Fonda was ahead of the times. In the early nineties, it started to be argued that men had been castrated by feminism, unable to value their masculinity. This was dubious as a theory (men may not have been valuing their masculinity, but neither were they helping with the housework much more than their masculine ancestors had) but Fonda was telling no more than the truth when she said that men had difficulty in dealing with powerful women, and she was one of the most powerful women in the world.

Ted Turner was many things that were of obvious attraction to Fonda. He had an air of southern chivalry, he was more powerful and considerably richer than she was ($1.6 billion to her $60 million, it was estimated), he had an international outlook deriving from his media interests that had certain resemblances to her liberalism, and he had his own strength, his own agenda.

When he first contacted her, she resisted, but by the time Fonda's divorce was going through at the end of 1989, they were

In Ted's view, Jane was not running for fitness, but 'away
from something'.

already a very visible couple. For the first time in her life, she became somebody's consort, accompanying Turner to his numerous public engagements and meetings with presidents and prime ministers. Fonda had a different, glossy, steely appearance, with startling dresses draped over her new breasts.

Just before Fonda's fifty-third birthday he gave her an engagement ring. They negotiated a pre-nuptial agreement in which she received $10 million of Turner Broadcasting stock but would have no claim on his estate, and on 21 December 1991, Jane Fonda's fifty-fourth birthday, they were married on his 8,000-acre Avalon Plantation in Florida. She wore a gown that she had worn in *Rollover*, and she was given away by her son, Troy.

Characteristically, Fonda announced that the truly important part of her life was just beginning: 'I firmly believe that we're at the perfect age to start over. There's so much that Ted and I can do to help make this a better planet for all of us. We're fortunate to have the tools.'

This involved certain changes in Fonda's life and career. In the early stages of her relationship with Turner there was still occasional talk of film projects, a life of Václav Havel, a screen version of Neil Sheehan's remarkable book about Vietnam, *A Bright Shining Lie*. But it quickly became clear to her that she would have to subordinate her career to his. This was reinforced in 1995 when Turner Broadcasting merged with Time Warner and Turner became vice-president of one of the largest communication companies in the world. Once again, the paradox: in order to achieve the goals she had set herself, she would have to become an old-fashioned wife. She certainly began to sound like one, or at least a post-feminist version. She said that younger friends had asked her how she could be married to this 'strong, domineering' man: 'I say you can be married to a strong man. There are times when you support him all the way and you recognise that in many ways he has pressures you'll never know. And he's more fragile, more prone to stress. Women should nurture and support that weakness in men. And yes, there are times when you give over to them.'

Fonda now seemed detached from her past, cooler in her appraisal of it. She never apologised for her radical youth – or middle-age – but instead began to treat it as if it were a necessary phase in a process of personal growth. She was at least plausible when she claimed that if it were not for this activism, then her energies would have had nowhere to go: 'Today I'd be a dyed blonde, a numb and dumb pill-popping star.' She kept a photograph of Marilyn Monroe on the wall of her office on the 20th Century Fox lot as an awful warning. 'If I hadn't taken up a cause, I could very well be dead like Marilyn. Not through drugs, but dead just the same. I keep her picture there to remind me how careful you have to be in this business not to go under.' Her trekking round army bases, posing by North Vietnamese anti-aircraft guns, was justified because it had helped ease the pressures of being a movie star. It is doubtful whether that argument was much comfort to the ex-prisoners-of-war in the Hanoi Hilton.

Her activism was not the only part of her life that was drastically reappraised. It now emerged that, far from being a part of the solution, her fitness routines had been part of the problem. 'I was hopelessly addicted to exercise,' she told a magazine at the beginning of 1996. 'I worked out two or three hours a day and took four-hour bike rides. Ted used to say, "You're not running for fitness, you're running away from something."' Under his influence, she had

Fonda remains a public figure, here speaking at a pro-choice
abortion rally in Washington D.C. in 1992.

Fonda startles Hollywood at the 1989 Oscars: a new man,
a new image, a new body.

changed to a kinder, gentler form of exercise, and she revealed that she was putting this new easier philosophy into a series of videos.

Nor was it just fitness that was damaging. From the vantage-point of retirement, Fonda could see that being a successful working woman had been harmful as well: 'Work defined me. I was successful, but I failed at two marriages.' Ted Turner wouldn't allow such distractions, and, she said, he wasn't afraid to ask for intimacy: 'I'm astounded by how many ways I still find to avoid it. But Ted tugs on my kite strings and pulls me back whenever I start to drift. Ted was real upfront. He said: "I need you here."'

And she was there. She could still be controversial, but when she accused Rupert Murdoch of bribing Rudolph Giuliani, the Majoy of New York City, by hiring Giuliani's wife, it was a salvo in her husband's bitter dispute with Murdoch over their rival cable news channels.

In the first five years of their marriage, the longest period they spent apart was six days, which is proof in itself that Fonda was no longer working as a movie actress. She is still a saleswoman in her own right. Her 1994 Walk to the Music Fitness Tread 'infomercial', which was shown on shopping TV networks, was reputedly the most successful fitness and health launch of the year, generating $130 million of sales, and this without Fonda ever being seen using the Music Fitness Tread – because she would have needed to rehearse and that would have meant being away from Turner for too long.

This latest stage of her life has proved to be different from her previous, essentially public existence. Her progress had always left a wake of resentment behind it, from spurned or abandoned supporters as much as enemies, and her feminist ex-colleagues who helped her break up the patriarchy of the FTA organisation might

Jane Fonda: still famous
after all these years –
and still controversial.

A life led in public: Jane
Fonda networks with
Maria Shriver and Arnold
Schwarzenegger.

complain that she was now allowing herself to be defined by a man. If this is so, then it was done as always with open eyes. Is this, she might have replied, any different from allowing herself to be defined by the political causes she pursued, by the roles she played, by the image of health and fitness she created?

Jane Fonda has always had a knack for deciding what is right for her and then going at it with a commitment that takes it further than even her friends and colleagues might have wanted. She then derives a philosophy from her particular experience. To juxtapose her different opinions at different times is rather like comparing a calendar at different times and criticising it for being inconsistent. It is in its nature to be so.

Jane Fonda's career has been magnificently managed but it is difficult not to regret the career that seemed in store for her after *They Shoot Horses, Don't They?* and *Klute,* and that never happened. In retrospect, this is partly a result of choices she made but it should be said that she isn't alone in this failure. In the sixties and early seventies, movie stars (most of them male) secured a degree of power that no screen actors had ever possessed before. What did they do with it? Warren Beatty was thirty when he made *Bonnie and Clyde* in 1967. In the following thirty years he made eleven films, of which perhaps three (all made by 1975) were worthwhile. Some might add *Reds* to this short list. Compare this with the record of James Stewart. Between the ages of thirty (in 1938) and sixty, Stewart made some forty films of which at least twenty are classics. (He also flew thirty bombing missions over Nazi Germany.) Beatty was a beneficiary of the shift in the financial structure of Hollywood, but were we as film-goers the losers? Much the same could be said of other highly intelligent, principled actors like Paul Newman or Robert Redford. (An interesting exception is Clint Eastwood, who has worked himself like a contract player, built up a remarkable range of good films *and* had a more successful political career than Tom Hayden.)

Jane Fonda arouses both the mixed feelings people have for politicians and the mixed feelings they have for powerful women. Most other film actresses are a part of our lives and we give them a meaning that becomes more poignant as their careers fade along with their looks. They are passive, preferably victims, and are symbols both of sexual glamour and of the pain of loss, of the passing of time. We look at Rita Hayworth and we sigh as we think of that gorgeousness that was captured on screen, and we ponder its brevity, and we contemplate the disaster of her life, her long, agonising decline, and we reflect on the passing of time and feel better about ourselves. Jane Fonda doesn't make us feel like that. She had the youthful beauty, then left it behind deliberately and went on to something else, and then something else and then something else again. Other female movie stars seem to need us to make them complete, but Jane Fonda doesn't need us, or if she does, it is only for a short time before she has moved on and left us behind. As the female political activist states ruefully in Robert Patrick's 1977 play *Kennedy's Children*: 'Did we march just to make Jane Fonda a star?'

Fonda represents many different things to different people – sexual freedom, physical fitness, conscience, treason – but what she represents to me is ceaseless energy. There's a horrible moment in *Klute* when she is in the throes of a fake orgasm with a client and she snatches a glimpse at her watch. There's an edginess about our relationship with Jane Fonda. Those who have crossed her path seem to have experienced it. Donald Sutherland, who loved her and was abandoned by her, recalled it with awe: 'Jane's personality is more

Jane Fonda: adored, admired, imitated,
envied, reviled, unforgiven.

Jane Fonda, triumphant at sixty.

specific than most of us. She's well disciplined and knows what she wants and where she's going and works objectively to apply all her information to that intention.' We get a hint of this even when we watch her on the screen. She is thinking hard, planning ahead, calculating, and even when she is performing for you, cajoling you to stretch those buttock muscles, urging you to better yourself, singing songs with the Vietcong, being as wonderful as she always is, just when she has her arms around your neck you wonder if she is doing it in order to get a glimpse of her wristwatch, because you suspect that she probably has somewhere else to go.

FILMOGRAPHY

Tall Story
1960; written by Julius J. Epstein, directed by Joshua Logan.

Walk on the Wild Side
1962; written by John Fante and Edmund Morris, directed by Edward Dmytryk.

The Chapman Report
1962; written by Wyatt Cooper and Don M. Mankiewicz, directed by George Cukor.

Period of Adjustment
1962; written by Isobel Lennart, directed by George Roy Hill.

In the Cool of the Day
1963; written by Meade Roberts, directed by Robert Stevens.

Sunday in New York
1964; written by Norman Krasna, directed by Peter Tewksbury.

Les Félins (*Joy House*)
1964; written and directed by René Clément.

Fonda the ingenue, when she was still
just a movie star.

La Ronde (*Circle of Love*)
1964; written by Jean Anouilh, directed by Roger Vadim.

Cat Ballou
1965; written by Walter Newman and Frank R. Pierson, directed by Elliot Silverstein.

The Chase
1966; written by Lillian Hellman, directed by Arthur Penn.

Any Wednesday
1966; written by Julius J. Epstein, directed by Robert Ellis Miller.

La Curée (*The Game is Over*)
1966; written by Jean Cau, Bernard Frechtman and Roger Vadim, directed by Roger Vadim.

Hurry Sundown
1966; written by Horton Foote and Thomas C. Ryan, directed by Otto Preminger.

Barefoot in the Park
1967; written by Neil Simon, directed by Gene Saks.

Histoires extraordinaires
the **Metzengerstein** episode (*Spirits of the Dead*; *Tales of Mystery*)
1967; written and directed by Roger Vadim.

Barbarella

1968; written by Terry Southern in collaboration with Claude
Brûlé, Jean-Claude Forest, Clement Biddle Wood, Tudor Gates,
Vittorio Bonicelli, Brian Degas and Roger Vadim, directed by
Roger Vadim.

They Shoot Horses, Don't They?

1969; written by Robert E. Thompson, directed by Sydney Pollack.

Klute

1971; written by Andy K. Lewis and Dave Lewis, directed by
Alan J. Pakula.

FTA

1972; written by Jane Fonda, Donald Sutherland, Dalton Trumbo,
Robin Menken, Rita Martinson, Michael Alaimo, Len Chandler,
Pamela Donegan and Holly Near, directed by Francine Parker.

Steelyard Blues

1972; written by David S. Ward, directed by Alan Myerson.

Tout va bien

1973; written by Jean-Luc Godard and Jean-Pierre Gorin, directed
by Jean-Luc Godard.

A Doll's House

1973; written by David Mercer, directed by Joseph Losey.

Introduction to the Enemy

1974; documentary by Jane Fonda, Tom Hayden and Haskell Wexler.

The Blue Bird

1976; written by Hugh Whitemore and Alfred Hayes, directed by George Cukor.

Fun with Dick and Jane

1977; written by Jerry Belson, Mordecai Richler and David Giler, directed by Ted Kotcheff.

Julia

1977; written by Alvin Sargent, directed by Fred Zinneman.

Coming Home

1978; written by Robert C. Jones and Waldo Salt, directed by Hal Ashby.

Comes a Horseman

1978; written by Dennis Lynton Clark, directed by Alan J. Pakula.

California Suite

1978; written by Neil Simon, directed by Herbert Ross.

The China Syndrome

1979; written by Mike Gray, T.S. Cook and James Bridges, directed by James Bridges.

~ Filmography ~

The Electric Horseman
1979; written by Robert Garland, directed by Sydney Pollack.

Nine to Five
1980; written by Patricia Resnick and Colin Higgins, directed by Colin Higgins.

On Golden Pond
1981; written by Ernest Thompson, directed by Mark Rydell.

Rollover
1981; written by David Shaber, directed by Alan J. Pakula.

Agnes of God
1985; written by John Pielmeier, directed by Norman Jewison.

The Morning After
1986; written by James Hicks, directed by Sidney Lumet.

Old Gringo
1989; written by Luis Puenzo and Aida Bortnik, directed by Luis Puenzo.

Stanley and Iris
1989; written by Irving Ravetch and Harriet Frank, Jnr, directed by Martin Ritt.

INDEX

ACKNOWLEDGMENTS

All Action: pp. 9, 24, 168, 172, 178 top, 182;

Associated Press: pp. 89, 105, 131 bottom, 144;

Camera Press: pp. 14, 17, 19, 32, 38, 53, 62, 85, 129, 184;

Corbis-Bettmann: pp. 23, 176; Corbis-Bettmann/Reuter:

p. 170; Corbis-Bettmann/UPI pp. 11, 20, 59 top, 178 bottom;

Corbis/Everett: p. 2; Hulton Getty: pp. 21, 70, 78, 102, 106,

124, 131 top, 137, 138 bottom, 175; Gary S. Franklin/Hulton:

p. 165; Kobal Collection: pp. 6, 12, 26, 29 top, 34, 44, 47, 49,

56, 59 bottom, 61, 65, 66, 69, 72, 75, 81, 92, 96, 98, 111, 115,

116, 120, 124, 135, 138 top, 148, 153, 155, 157, 158, 161,

163; Scope Features: p. 29 bottom